# ABOUT WAYNE HARRISON

- Ex-Professional Player with Blackpool; England and Oulu Palloseura; Finland
- Represented Great Britain in the World Student Games in Mexico
- Bachelors of Arts in Sports Psychology
- UEFA 'A' License 1996
- NSCAA Premier Diploma holder
- Author of 14 Coaching Books and 4 DVD's
- DOC for Al Ain Soccer Club; United Arab Emirates; Middle East; 7 Youth National Championships in 2 years at Professional level
- Proponent of Soccer Awareness One Touch Developmental Training
- Owner Soccer Awareness Developmental Training programs

## Teaching Rondos Using the Soccer Awareness Philosophy of Player Development

Pep Guardiola quoted this about rondos at Barcelona: "What I learnt here is everything starts with the ball and ends with the ball. Sometimes we forget that it's a game of 11 v 11 with ONE BALL. We try to keep this ball, we try to play with this ball, we try to make everything with the ball. This is what we learn when we start as children there."

### What is Soccer Awareness?

"The ultimate goal in coaching is helping each player develop his or her talents and abilities to the fullest. With this in mind, I created this Unique Soccer Awareness philosophy of developmental coaching and training. It simply means training the mind before the body." - Wayne Harrison

We will show the link between Soccer Awareness and what rondos teach in this book.

### The link between our Soccer Awareness Continuums of Development Model and using Rondos to highlight the skills taught in them

The following is a guide as to what goes on in a players head, before, during and after receiving the ball. All these thoughts processes translate into physical actions on the field. Many decisions are made before the player even gets the ball, this is the essence of Soccer Awareness teaching and shown in the Continuums model.

When you assess what Rondos teach you will see this continuum highlights the very same actions learnt. Rondos are ideal training for this "thinking process" because everything has to be done at pace with little time to think and assess so players are forced to make very quick decisions which in turn forces them to think AHEAD of the ball before they receive it.

Soccer Awareness training and Rondos go hand in hand in their education of players.

# Continuums of Development Evaluation Form

## RATING:

6: Excellent
5: Strength
4: Good
3: Average
2: Needs Improvement
1: Needs Much Work to Improve

## Word Association combining thought and deed

A, B, C and D, has to be determined BEFORE the player receives the ball.

"Look and Think" MUST come first before everything else, then its: LOOK / THINK / ACT / SUCCEED.

## The Continuum and it's actions:

A) LOOK / OBSERVE / THINK (BEFORE receiving the ball; assessing all options in "Anticipation" not as a Reaction) If time allows take 2 or 3 looks because the situation may have changed

B) SKILL: THE DECISION (How, why; when and where of Technique; plus its success or not; and why?)

C) FOOT PREPARATION / BODY POSITION (flat footed, off balance?)

D) COMMUNICATION (Verbal and visual)

E) CONTROL (If not a one touch pass on, the 1st touch control)

F) TECHNIQUE (the pass, the run, the dribble, the turn, the shot; etc.)

G) TACTICAL MOBILITY (Movement off the ball, finding space; 90% of the game)

H) MENTAL TRANSITION (Possession changes, Player tunes in immediately?)

**The decision making thought process of the player about to receive the ball at any one moment is as follows**

1. Observe where the ball is coming from.

2. Observe how the ball is coming (on the ground, in the air).

3. Know where teammates are before receiving the ball

4. Know where the opposition players are before receiving the ball.

5. Know where the important SPACE is for the next move before receiving the ball

6. Before the ball arrives, get both feet into the correct position and the body in the Correct position to receive it.

7. Decide "what" to do with the ball. (technique / skill to use (emphasis on a good first Touch) - pass, run, shoot, cross, dribble, dummy / leave. (What are the options?). Narrow the list of possible outcomes from all options

7. Observe "where" the ball is to be moved, passed or played. Can be based on where you are on the field of play. (Assess open spaces and supporting options on the field).

8. Decide "when" the ball goes. (the timing of the technique / skill)

9. Decide "how" the ball goes. (the selection of the technique / skill used)

10. Decide "why" the ball goes. (Compare all options with the team's tactical objectives)

**This is what we will teach the players thru the Continuums Model of Development:**

1. Looking before receiving the ball
2. Looking away from the ball as well as at it
3. Knowing options in advance of receiving
4. Weighting the pass correctly to help the receiver
5. Getting their foot preparation right (how many play flat footed?? This won't let them if they want to be successful).
6. Getting their body shape right, facing where the next pass is going; in advance of the ball
7. Getting into position quickly "Off the ball" to help the player receiving; and it has to be before the receiver gets the ball as they only have one touch to move it on again either to feet or to space

They will recognize if the fault and failure to maintain possession was in the weight of the receiving pass, or in the next first touch pass by the receiver, or because of poor off the ball support or even the bad bounce of the field. It is not difficult to identify which it is. It will not be because of pressure or interceptions by defenders because in the early stages there will not be any defenders so the players can play without pressure.

**A One Touch Mentality:**

What does it mean? It means every player thinks like they only have ONE touch; to "force" them to observe the field and their BEST option BEFORE they receive the ball. When they receive it the resulting decision may already actually be the opposite to One touch; maybe to dribble, to pass using 2 or 3 touches, to slow the game down and change the TEMPO, to run with the ball; or Even to play ONE TOUCH.

We build this mentality into the Rondos we use.

# The Importance of Developing Players Through Teaching Rondos

Welcome to this book exploring the use of rondos in youth soccer.

I have included as a way to work into these game situations many Rondo ideas I feel are great foundation builders for players learning to combine and play together.

I have stayed with simplistic ideas that all levels of players can try and be successful at, it is up to each coach to work out how to make it work for their players.

Though the foundation of the basic rondo stays the same, we explore different ways to present it.

It can be made easier or more difficult based on the number of touches players are allowed for example so it benefits ALL players who practice with them; also the size of area they play within can be manipulated to change the challenge.

Rondos are a great way; in my opinion; to prepare players for the game situations and especially the fast decision making needed within the game.

## What do Rondos Teach?

A rondo for example isn't just 4 players playing keep away from a single player and a bit of fun (though they Are fun), what you get out of a rondo is the following:

1. Soccer Awareness: Assessing options BEFORE receiving the ball: The Think and Look

2. Technique,

3. Mobility,

4. Agility and balance

5. Body position,

6. Foot preparation,

7. Communication,

8. The 1st touch,

9. The 2nd touch, and beyond

10. Teamwork,

11. Collective tactical understanding in a small sided game environment,

12. Positioning OFF the ball,

13. Problem solving,

14. And developing creativity and imagination,

15. Intensity of play,

16. Physically challenging;

17. Developing Angles of support;

18. Opening up passing lanes by movement off the ball;

19. Speeding up thinking and decision making, The SKILL FACTOR;

20. Ultimately providing a competitive environment where no one wants to give the ball away and finally,

21. They are fun to do.

**An example of how we develop a Soccer Awareness Rondo over time and increase the challenges**

The following diagrams show the basic Rondo we begin with.  It is none pressured, unlimited touches, and presented in a simple way to allow the players to easily begin the process of education. It is the attention to detail that is paramount in the learning process. The Ball must  be passed around the square not across it. Players adjust their position based on the ball. They use the cones as positional points of reference.

Players MUST always open up their body stance to receive with their BACK FOOT. Ways to build the Rondo and increase challenges:

1.  Playing unlimited touches
2.  Playing 3 touches
3.  Playing two touches;
4.  Playing one touch when able but  2 touches maximum
5.  Adding a defender in the middle so 4 v 1 (can again go back to unlimited touches, 3, then 2, then 1 when able so many more progressions just within the 4 v 1 itself).
6.  Players change position and rotate on the outside
7.  Add another defender, now 4 v 2 (number of touches, size of area change etc)
8.  Challenge outside player to split the 2 defenders with a pass between them
9.  Add a neutral attacking player in the middle who outside players MUST involve consistently so now 4 v 2 plus 1. Neutral player 3 or 2 touches only
10. Neutral player ONE touch only
11. Neutral player can rotate in and out with outside players; so very fast decision making in rotations of players added to the passing itself.
12. Reduce to a 3 v 1 rondo and assess if the players are ready to play 1 or 2 touches yet. A very fast movement off the ball challenge now
13. Decrease the size of the grid so less space, faster decisions needed; tighter passing lanes to find, better soccer awareness required.
14. Can you think of any other progressions you could add to this to increase the challenge and intensity of the practice?
15. Once players are EXCELLENT at all these progressions a logical move now would be to go to double rondos.  More players, more options, more decisions, and now mental transitions happen more going from attacking to defending at pace

# Contents

## Introduction to Playing 4 v 4 Using Rondos

The USSF now have made it mandatory for 4 v 4 games to be played at the younger ages. This is a GREAT MOVE and long overdue.

This is what US Youth Soccer states:

Here are some of the reasons why we believe, as soccer coaches, administrators and parents must guarantee that our young soccer players play small-sided games:

1. Because we want our young soccer players to touch the soccer ball more often and become more skillful with it! (Individual technical development)

2. Because we want our young soccer players to make more, less-complicated decisions during the game! (Tactical development)

3. Because we want our young soccer players to be more physically efficient in the field space they are playing in! (Reduced field size)

4. Because we want our young soccer players to have more individual teaching time with the coach! Fewer players on the field and fewer players on the team will guarantee this! (Need to feel worthy and need to feel important)

5. Because we want our young soccer players to have more, involved playing time in the game! (More opportunity to solve problems that only the game presents)

6. Because we want our young soccer players to have more opportunity to play on both sides of the ball! (More exposure to attacking and defending situations)

7. Because we want our young soccer players to have more opportunities to score goals! (Pure excitement)

8. Because we want to include children of all temperaments, assertive to shy, to have more opportunities to interact with others and the game! (Socialization)

These are the reasons why we adults must foster "Small-Sided Games" in our youth soccer programs. The "Small-Sided" environment is a developmentally appropriate environment for our young soccer players. It's a FUN environment that focuses on the young soccer player.

All makes total common sense.

# Quick Transition 2 V 2 Rondos With Players Staying In Their Own Zones
## An Introduction to 4 v 4 Rondos

1. A 2 v 2 game going to 4 goals. The team who scores stays on and must quickly defend the 2 new players coming in (one from each goal that the opposition defends).

2. Instant transition with the same ball that the opponents scored with, here (3) and (4) are positioned to immediately bring the ball the opponents' may score with out to attack. The other two players (1) and (2) must get off the field ASAP.

3. Introduce a target player (can be coaches or players). Now it can be a 3 v 2 effectively.

Players can use the target to play give and goes with each other or with their immediate teammates.

## Coaching Points Attacking:

1. Quick Break and counter attack

2. Switching the point of attack if another goal is more open

3. Quick one and two touch passing

4. Positioning to open up passing lanes and getting between defenders to pass the ball in early

5. Creating 2 v 1 situations from a 2 v 2 set up and setting up a give and go.

## Coaching Points Defending:

1. Instant pressure as possession changes (transition after scoring going from being an attacker to being a defender)

2. Regaining possession at the front with a scoring reward

3. Getting in front of the passing lanes to prevent the quick pass into the goal.

4. Working together with pressure and support, the support player supporting the first defender, stepping across and covering the passing lane to the second goal and also keeping an eye on the 2nd attacker.

## Transition Coaching Points:

Immediately the team that has been in possession of the ball and has scored then they must switch on mentally to being defenders and high pressuring the new attacking team to try to win the ball back and score again.

# Quick Transition 2 v 2 Rondos

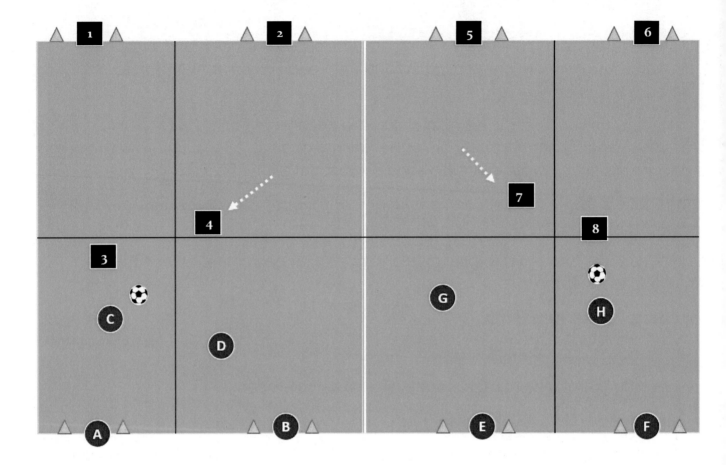

1. A 2 v 2 game going to 2 goals. The team who scores stays on and must quickly defend the 2 new players coming in (one from each goal that the opposition defends). (3) PRESSES AND (4) CUTS OFF THE PASSING LANE TO GOAL

2. Offside half way line. Instant transition with the same ball that the opponents scored with.

3. Players can use the target to play give and goes with each other or with their immediate teammates.

# Quick Transition 2 v 2 Rondos

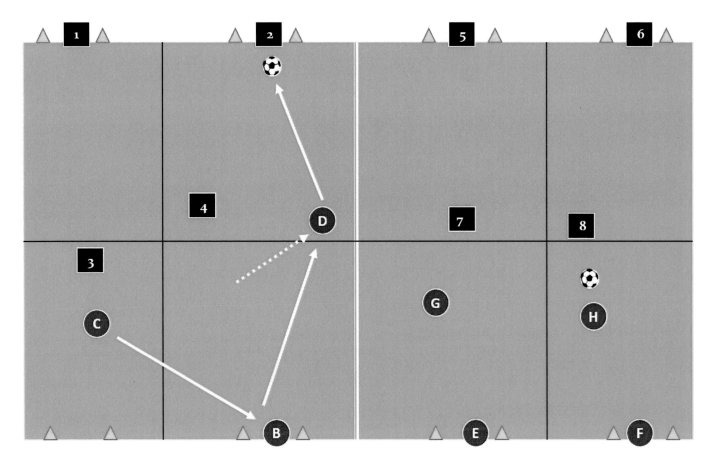

1. Use the players in the goals to support. They have 1 or 2 touches only so they must play quickly.

2. Now it is essentially a 3 v 2. For the inside players start with unlimited touches then as they are successful decrease the number to test their peripheral vision and awareness on and off the ball.

3. Always increasing the challenge each point of success is reached.

# Now develop by allowing the balls to transfer

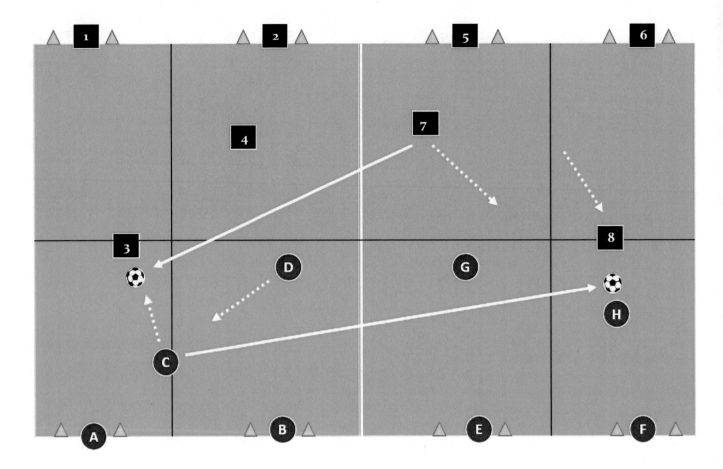

1. This will really test the players imagination and awareness on and off the ball. In one instant (3) and (4) are defending, in the next they are attacking. Likewise for the letters team.

2. Here we show how the mental transition works with each team suddenly changing their positions defensively to deal with the change.

# Quick Transition 2 v 2 Rondos / An Introduction to 4 v 4 Rondos

1. A 2 v 2 game going to 4 goals. The team who scores stays on and must quickly defend the 2 new players coming in (one from each goal that the opposition defends).
2. Instant transition with the same ball that the opponents scored with, here (3) and (4) are positioned to immediately bring the ball the opponents' may score with out to attack. The other two players (1) and (2) must get off the field ASAP.
3. Introduce a target player (can be coaches or players). Now it can be a 3 v 2 effectively. Players can use the target to play give and goes with each other or with their immediate teammates.
4. Liken passing into the goal as a midfielder passing into a striker so they get the ball in there as quickly as possible or a defender into a midfielder.

The 1st thought of the player on the ball has to be "Can I score?" The 1st thought of the 1st defender is can I stop them scoring, win possession immediately, and score myself. First team to 10 goals wins, keeping the competitive element. If the ball goes out of play the coach can provide another one to keep things going quickly.

## Coaching Points Attacking:

1. Quick Break and counter attack
2. Switching the point of attack if another goal is more open
3. Quick one and two touch passing
4. Positioning to open up passing lanes and getting between defenders to pass the ball in early
5. Creating 2 v 1 situations from a 2 v 2 set up and setting up a give and go.

## Coaching Points Defending:

1. Instant pressure as possession changes (transition after scoring going from being an attacker to being a defender)
2. Regaining possession at the front with a scoring reward
3. Getting in front of the passing lanes to prevent the quick pass into the goal.
4. Working together with pressure and support, the support player supporting the first defender, stepping across and covering the passing lane to the second goal and also keeping an eye on the 2nd attacker.

## Transition Coaching Points:

Immediately the team that has been in possession of the ball and has scored then they must switch on mentally to being defenders and high pressuring the new attacking team to try to win the ball back and score again.

# Quick Transition 2 v 2 Rondos

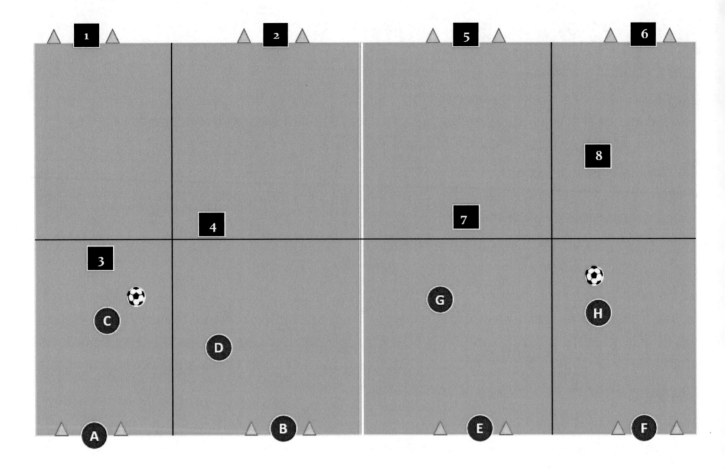

1. A 2 v 2 game going to 2 goals. The team who scores stays on and must quickly defend the 2 new players coming in (one from each goal that the opposition defends).

2. Offside half way line. Instant transition with the same ball that the opponents scored with.

3. Players can use the target to play give and goes with each other or with their immediate teammates.

# Quick Transition 4 v 4 Rondos

This activity begins as a 4 v 4 game working on zonal marking (marking space). Use a rope (Orange lines in diagram) to tie the players together so they have to move as a unit and so they "feel it". It can be a back four or a midfield four - the responsibilities are the same.

Four 2-yard wide goals are created with cones for each team to defend as shown.

Teams can score in any goal at any time. Each team must work in a unit of four (or a three with three goals to defend). Each goal is zoned off for a player to fill.

**Explanation:** To maintain a shape players defend their own goals but must support their team-mates to regain possession. By focusing on a goal of their own to defend it helps them keep a sense of shape as a unit.

They have to think about defending their goal, keeping their zone, supporting the pressing player and marking their own player who is in their zone.

Players must try to maintain their shape and not be moved around by the opposition as they would if they were man-marking players not space.

Players must squeeze centrally behind the ball. To establish where zones begin and end, place cones down to represent boundaries.

Note - Players take their shape from 4 references, the rope, the zone; the goal; the opposing players.

# Quick Transition 4 v 4 Rondos (Defending)

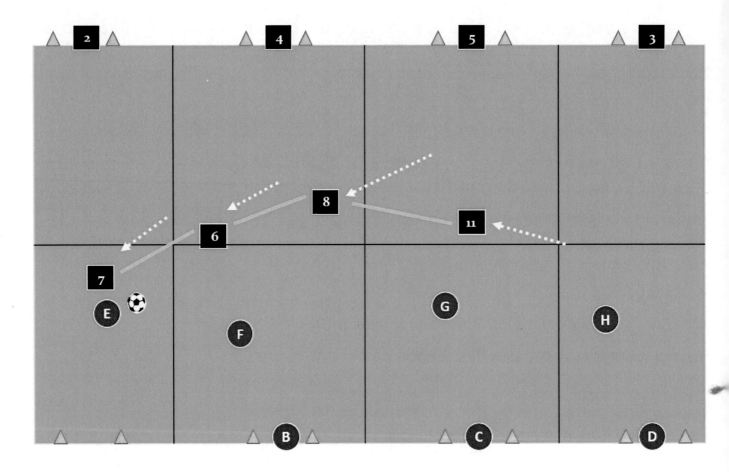

1. A 4 v 4 game going to 4 goals. The team who scores stays on and must quickly defend the 4 new players coming in (one from each goal that the opposition defends).

2. Offside half way line. Instant transition with the same ball that the opponents scored with.

3. Players can use the target to play give and goes with each other or with their immediate teammates.

# Quick Transition 4 v 4 Rondos (Defending)

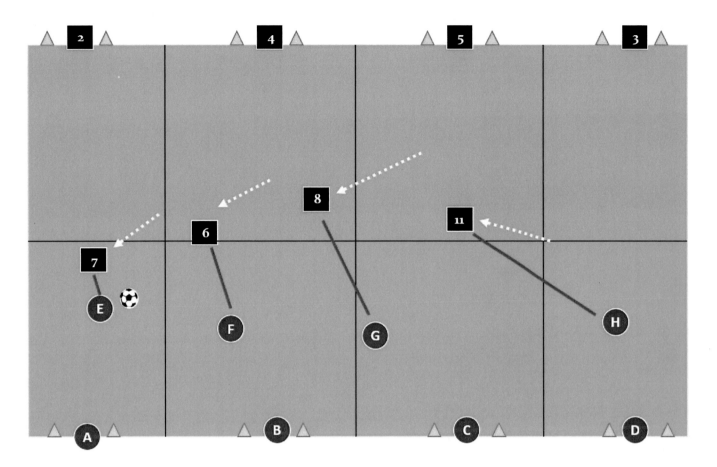

Here the players are illustrated "sliding" to squeeze the player on the ball as well as offer defensive balance and support. As the ball moves each player adjusts to become the pressing player (if it´s to their immediate opponent) or a support player who judges position from how close they are to the ball. The closer to the ball the more they mark the player the further from the ball the more they mark space.  As above (7) is closest, (6) and (8) are next closest and (11) is the furthest away but still close enough to close down as the ball travels. Introduce offside to make it more realistic. Distances shown by the blue lines.

# Quick Transition 4 v 4 Rondos (Defending)

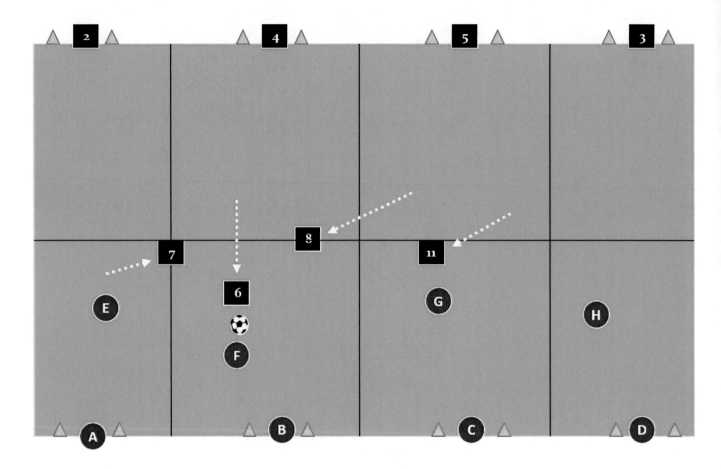

Here the ball is passed to (F) and the defenders adjust accordingly. They squeeze centrally behind the ball marking space but close enough in distance to close their immediate opponent down. For example (7) judges position by where the ball is and where the immediate opponent is so if the ball is passed to (H) there is time to close down and get to that player.

Show the positions of the players in relation to their own goals, can the opponent with the ball see the goal and score?

# Transition from attacking to defending

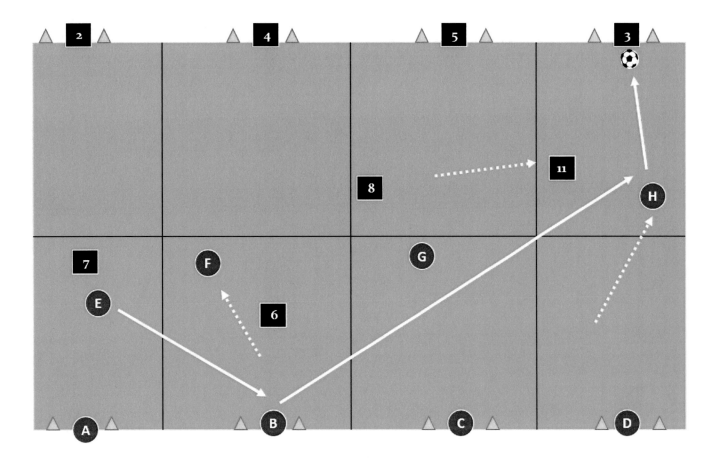

Using the support players enables the attacking team infield players to move forward. If (F) stays near (B) then they both do the same job so we need to use the 4 support players correctly to enable an 8 v 4 to develop.

6, 7, 8 and 11 drop out and 2, 3 , 4, and 5 come in and the letters team now must IMMEDIATELTY defend.

**Showing the Transition**

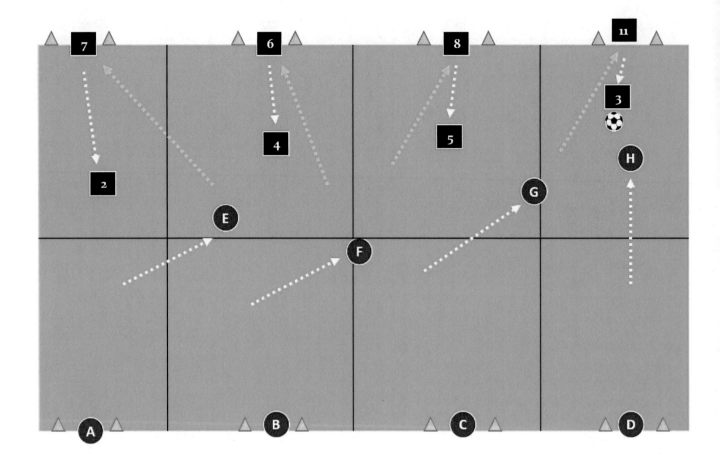

1. Here we show how the attacking team now has to adjust across to become the defending team INSTANTLY.

2. Yellow shows the route back for the transitioning team.

3. Attacking numbers team immediately condenses from playing wide and long (attacking shape) to short and tight (Defending shape).

# Quick Transition 4 v 4 Rondos (Attacking)

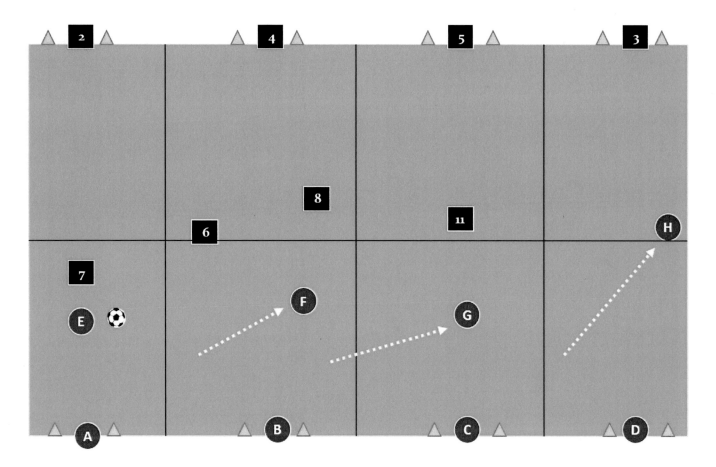

1. A 4 v 4 game going to 4 goals. The team who scores stays on and must quickly defend the 4 new players coming in (one from each goal that the opposition defends).

2. Offside half way line. Instant transition with the same ball that the opponents scored with.

3. Players can use the target to play give and goes with each other or with their immediate teammates.

# Quick Transition 4 v 4 Rondos (Attacking)

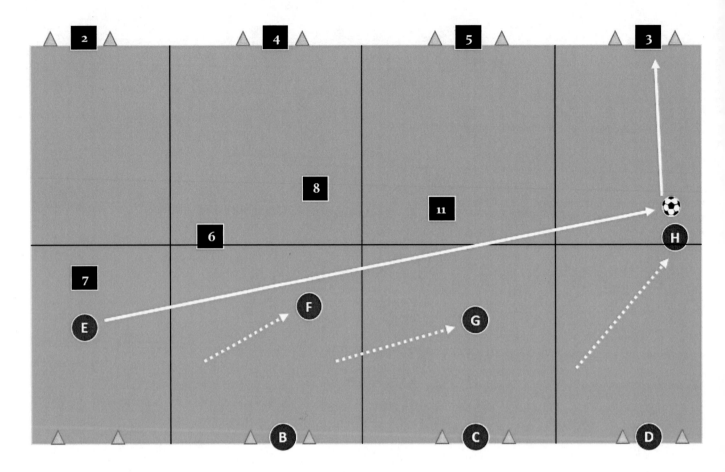

1. Attacking team wide and long, defending team short and tight. Attacking team MUST use the full space to gain the advantage.

2. The best move would be to transfer the ball quickly from (E) to (H) directly so the defending team might not have time to adjust to stop the attacking team. The switch of play means we score immediately.

# Quick Transition 4 v 4 Rondos (Attacking)

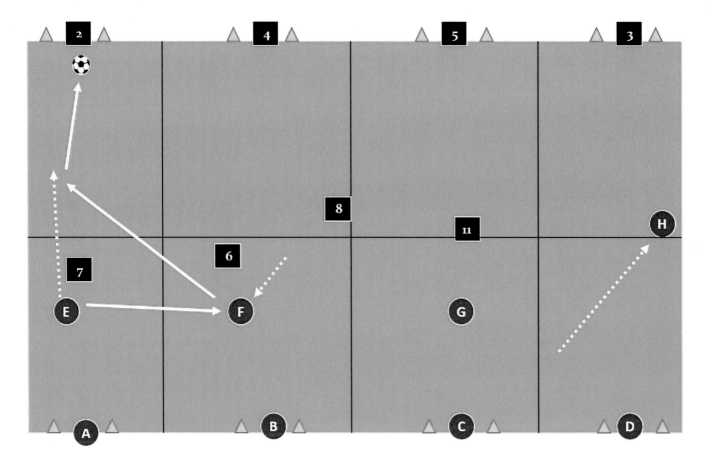

1. Playing give and goes. (F) drops off to receive in space and plays a give and go with (E) who gets in behind (7) staying onside and scoring.

2. Timing of the run and timing and angle of the pass must be in synch so (E) is not offside receiving the pass.

# Quick transition Overlap decoy runs

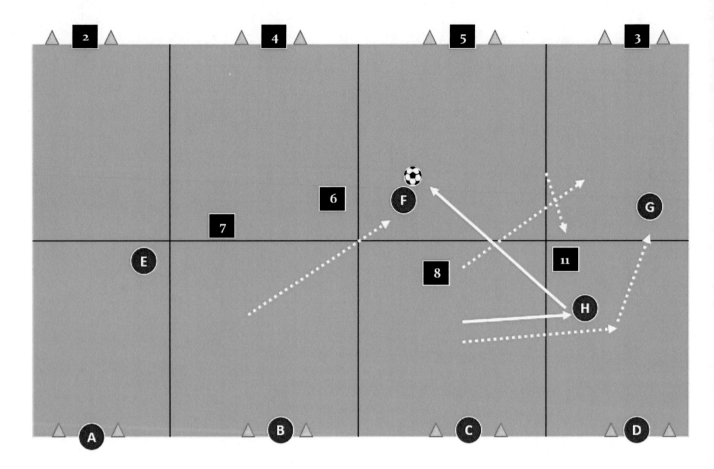

1. (G) passes to (H) and makes an overlap run that turns out to be a decoy run.

2. (8) tracks (G) and takes (8) out of an important space inside..

3. If this is done at pace it is very difficult to stop.

4. (F) makes a run inside of (6) from their Blind Side using (G)s run as a decoy and scores.

# Quick transition Third man run

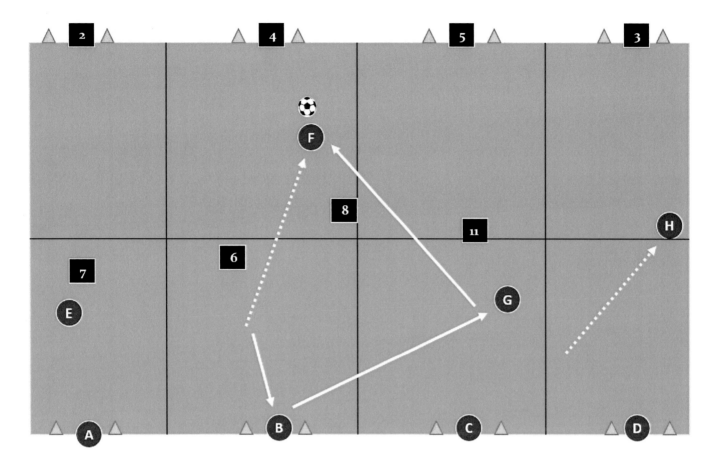

1. Using the support players in behind (F) pays the ball back to (B) who passes to (G) who plays (F) in behind the opponents defender making a third man run OFF the ball.

2. Timing of the run on the blind side of (8) must be such that (F) does not run offside before the ball is delivered.

3. Triangular support between the three players brings success.

## Quick Transition 6 v 6 Rondos (Attacking)

This activity begins as a 6 v 6 game working on zonal marking (marking space). Use a rope (Orange lines in diagram) to tie the players together so they have to move as a unit and so they "feel it". It can be a back four or a midfield four - the responsibilities are the same.

Four 2-yard wide goals are created with cones for each team to defend as shown.

Teams can score in any goal at any time. Each team must work in a unit of four (or a three with three goals to defend). Each goal is zoned off for a player to fill.

Area: 32 x 16

# Quick Transition 6 v 6 Rondos (Attacking)

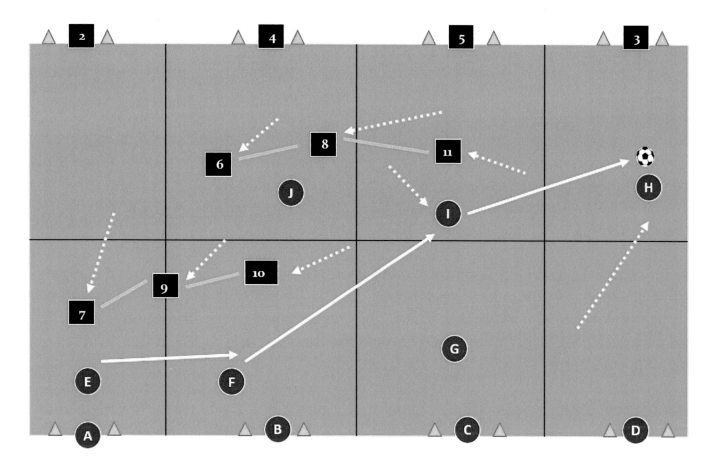

1. Switching the point of attack is vital here and it must be done as fast as possible so the defending team do not have time to adjust.

2. Now the attacking letters team on scoring immediate transition physically and mentality to defending.

## Quick Transition 6 v 6 Rondos (Defending)

This activity begins as a 6 v 6 game working on zonal marking (marking space). Use a rope (Orange lines in diagram) to tie the players together so they have to move as a unit and so they "feel it". It can be a back four or a midfield four - the responsibilities are the same.

Four 2-yard wide goals are created with cones for each team to defend as shown. Teams can score in any goal at any time. Each team must work in a unit of four (or a three with three goals to defend). Each goal is zoned off for a player to fill.

Area: 32 x 16

**Explanation:** To maintain a shape players defend their own goals but must support their team-mates to regain possession. By focusing on a goal of their own to defend it helps them keep a sense of shape as a unit. They have to think about defending their goal, keeping their zone, supporting the pressing player and marking their own player who is in their zone.

Players must try to maintain their shape and not be moved around by the opposition as they would if they were man-marking players not space. Players must squeeze centrally behind the ball. To establish where zones begin and end, place cones down to represent boundaries.

Note - Players take their shape from 4 references, the rope, the zone the goal the opposing players.

# Quick Transition 6 v 6 Rondos (Defending)

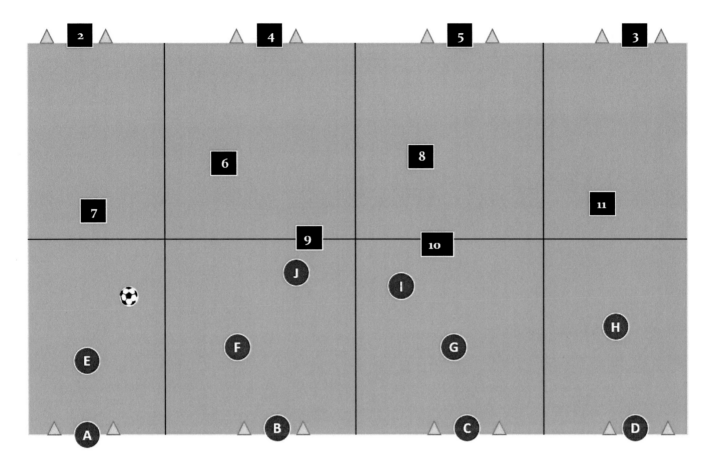

1. Introduce two more players per team each team can represent a back four plus two central strikers or a midfield four and two strikers. Again we are looking to maintain a team zonal marking shape.

2. Now we have a 6 v 6 rondo transition game, more players, more choices, more thinking required to work out solutions to problems offensively and defensively.

# Quick Transition 6 v 6 Rondos (Defending)

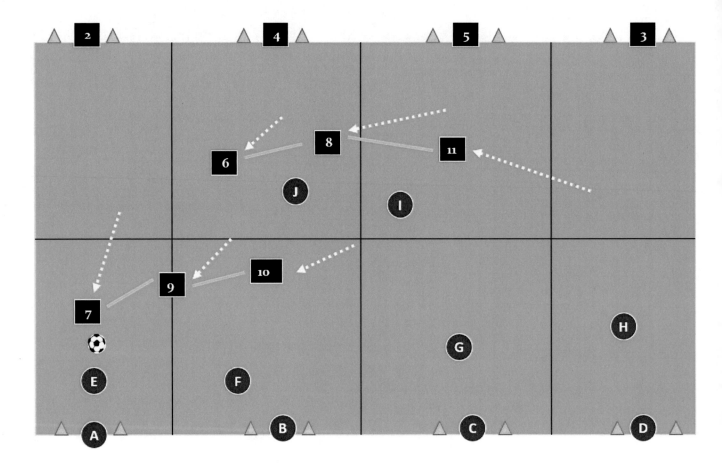

1. We are still trying to maintain a shape marking zones (spaces) but being aware of the immediate opponents' position.

2. The rope theory can be applied again here where they move in unison (2 midfield also). Use a rope (Orange lines in diagram) to tie the players together so they have to move as a unit and so they "feel it".

**Quick transition 3 v 3 Rondos with Players staying in their own zones. Teach this for using a back three.**

1. A 3 v 3 game going to 6 goals. The team who scores stays on and must quickly defend the 3 new players coming in (one from each goal that the opposition defends).

2. Staying in their own zones means this is very much 3 x 1 v 1s in each zone so working on 1 v 1 defending and 1 v 1 attacking but trying to create combination plays in attack also.

## Coaching Points Attacking:

1. Quick Break and counter attack

2. Switching the point of attack if another goal is more open

3. Quick one and two touch passing

4. Positioning to open up passing lanes and getting between defenders to pass the ball in early

5. Creating 2 v 1 or 3 v 2 situations from a 3 v 3 set up and setting up a give and go.

## Coaching Points Defending:

1. Instant pressure as possession changes (transition after scoring going from being an attacker to being a defender)

2. Regaining possession at the front with a scoring reward

3. Getting in front of the passing lanes to prevent the quick pass into the goal.

4. Working together with pressure and support, the support player supporting the first defender, stepping across and covering the passing lane to the second goal and also keeping an eye on the 2nd attacker as does the third defender and covering the third attacker.

## Transition Coaching Points:

Immediately the team that has been in possession of the ball and has scored then they must switch on mentally to being defenders and high pressuring the new attacking team to try to win the ball back and score again.

**Area:** 21 x 14

# Defending Quick Transition 3 v 3 Rondos

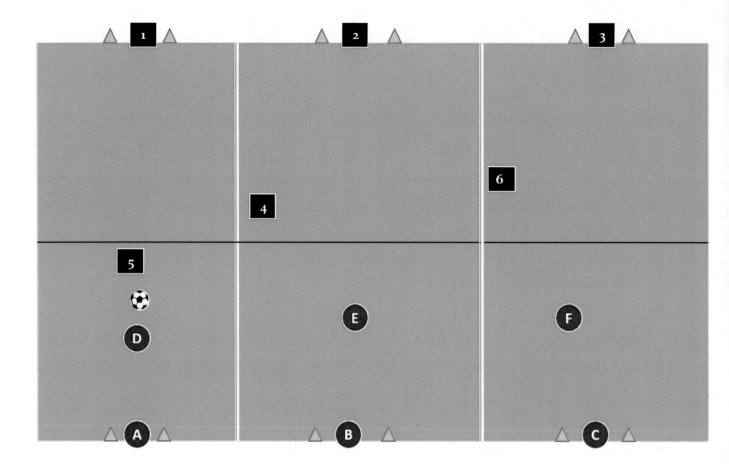

1. 3 v 3 game going to 6 goals. The team who scores stays on and must quickly defend the 3 new players coming in (one from each goal that the opposition defends).

2. Offside half way line. Instant transition with the same ball that the opponents scored with.

3. Players can use the target to play give and goes with each other or with their immediate teammates.

# Defending Quick Transition 3 v 3 Rondos

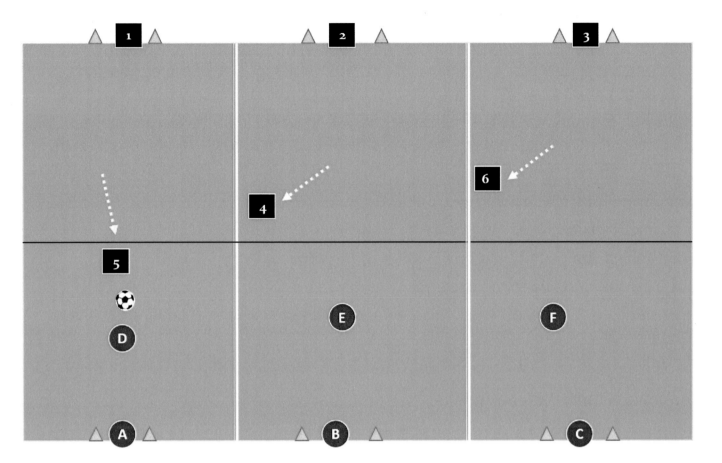

(5) Presses and (4) cuts off the passing lane to the middle goal. (6) gets as close to (4) to help as possible.    This is essentially 3 x 1 v 1s as player remain in their own zones.

**Quick transition 3 v 3 Rondos with Players moving throughout the zones. Teach this for using a back three.**

1. A 3 v 3 game going to 6 goals. The team who scores stays on and must quickly defend the 3 new players coming in (one from each goal that the opposition defends).

2. Staying in their own zones means this is very much 3 x 1 v 1s in each zone so working on 1 v 1 defending and 1 v 1 attacking but trying to create combination plays in attack also.

## Coaching Points Attacking:

1. Quick Break and counter attack

2. Switching the point of attack if another goal is more open

3. Quick one and two touch passing

4. Positioning to open up passing lanes and getting between defenders to pass the ball in early

5. Creating 2 v 1 or 3 v 2 situations from a 3 v 3 set up and setting up a give and go.

## Coaching Points Defending:

1. Instant pressure as possession changes (transition after scoring going from being an attacker to being a defender)

2. Regaining possession at the front with a scoring reward

3. Getting in front of the passing lanes to prevent the quick pass into the goal.

4. Working together with pressure and support, the support player supporting the first defender, stepping across and covering the passing lane to the second goal and also keeping an eye on the 2nd attacker as does the third defender and covering the third attacker.

## Transition Coaching Points:

Immediately the team that has been in possession of the ball and has scored then they must switch on mentally to being defenders and high pressuring the new attacking team to try to win the ball back and score again.

**Area:** 21 x 14

# Defending Quick Transition 3 v 3 Rondos

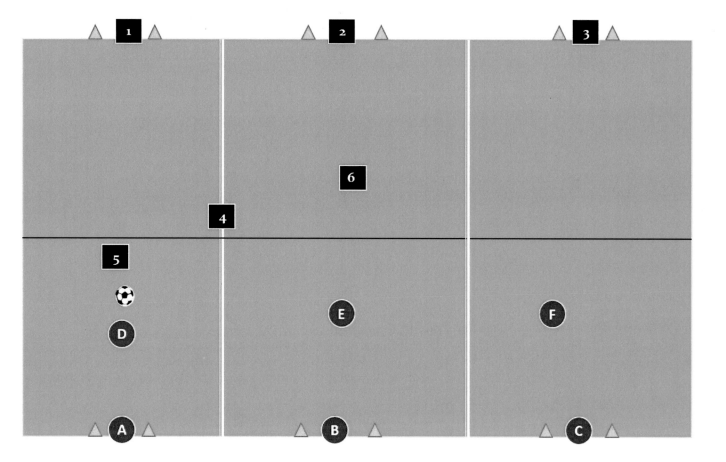

1. More realistic now. 3 v 3 game going to 6 goals. The team who scores stays on and must quickly defend the 3 new players coming in (one from each goal that the opposition defends).

2. Offside half way line. Instant transition with the same ball that the opponents scored with.

3. Players can use the target to play give and goes with each other or with their immediate teammates.

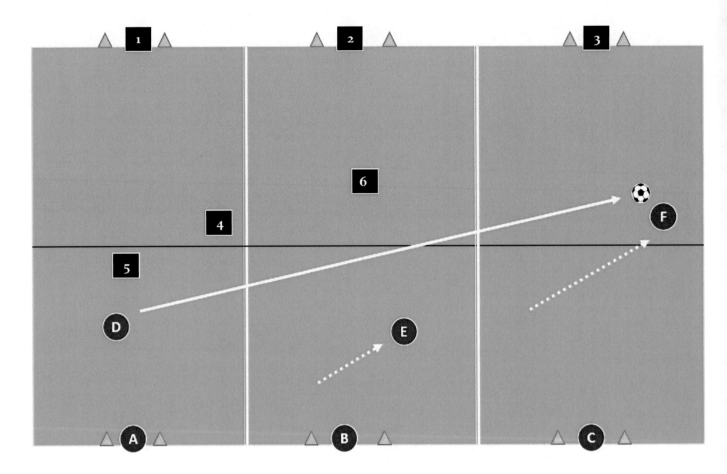

Attacking team get as wide and big as possible to open up the spaces between each other and make it more difficult to defend and for defenders to cover the open ground. Now (F) easily scores in goal 3.

## A Game Situational Soccer Awareness Rondo

A rondo can be applied on certain parts of the field of play.

The next exercise is based on the positioning of the players around Zone 14 (the zone in front of the opponents back 3 or 4 and their midfield).

Here we start the exercise off as a typical rondo and develop the idea to take it into the game situation.

This example can be the shape within a 4-2-3-1 system of play.

# An Attacking Team Shape Rondo

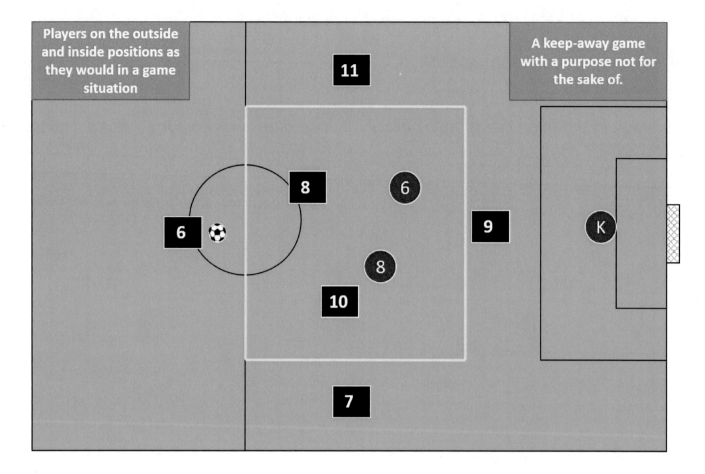

2 v 2. (8) and (10) keep the ball away from (6) and (8). They can use outside players as support and play two touches for speed of play. Defenders try to keep the ball if they win it.

The beauty of this rondo is it is game situational it is based on the team formation.

The rondo is set up as the team shape and it develops into rotational movements to confuse defenders.

# An Attacking Team Shape Drill With Interchanges

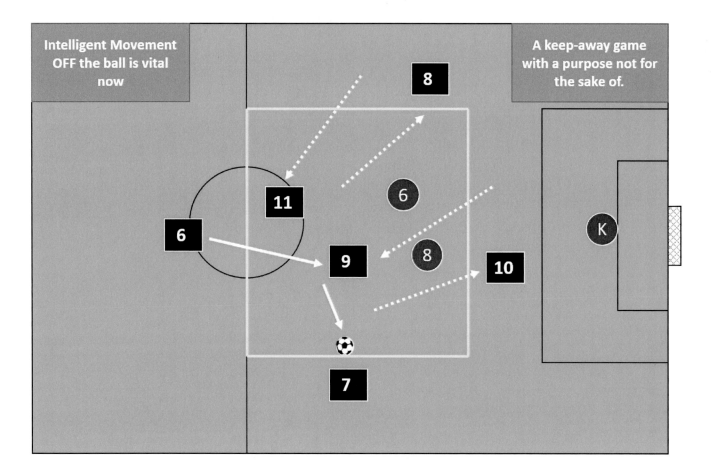

Players move in and out on the attacking team to confuse opponents. This is so much more than a typical posession game with players on the outside as each player moves based on the 4-2-3-1.

# An Attacking Team Shape Drill With Interchanges

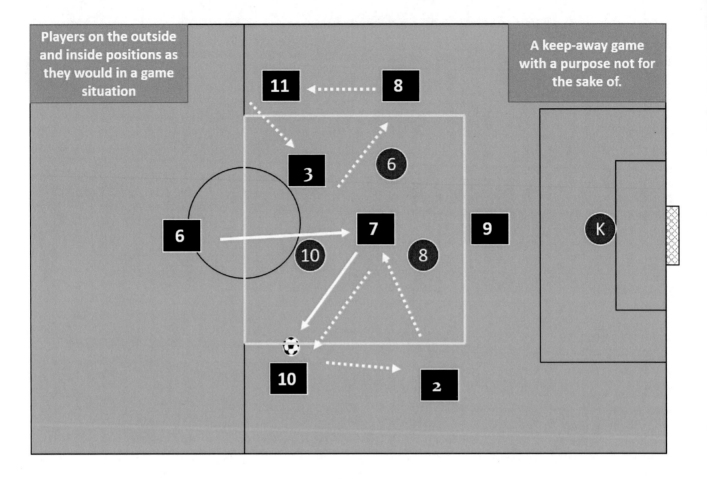

Add Wing backs (2) and (3). Introduce another defender to increase the pressure. Then make it a 2 v 4 against in the middle to really test the players. Players can rotate on the blind side of the ball.

# A Rondo Overloading Players in the Zone 14

This Rondo is perfect for a starting point on rotation and movement in fornt of opponents defense.

Teams may work out that we are good at playing penetrating passes and making great runs in behind them so the way to try to stop this is to defend deep.

If they defend deep we need a tactical solution to counter this.

This presentation gives you ideas on how to do this and play initially IN-FRONT of the opponents back four.

Bayern Munich and Barcelona are very good at this, both motivated and taught by Pep Guardiola.

We can do it at our age level just as effectively.

We can practice this in a tight area, with the relevant players in their usual positions in the attacking third and just play possession as a warm up.

## Setting conditions to make it work

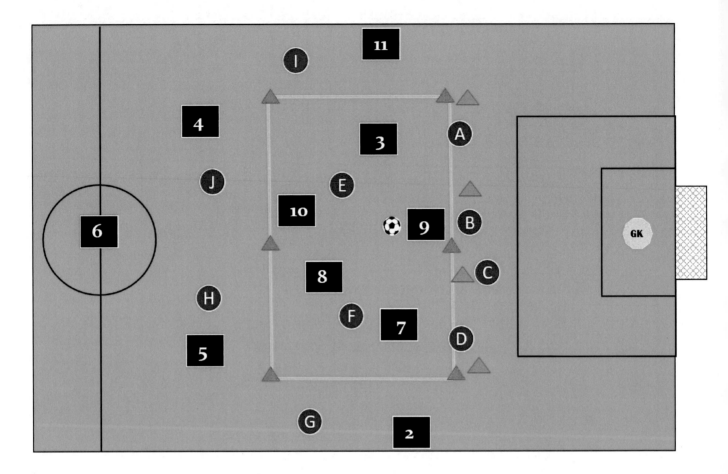

We overload zone 14 as shown. Condition the back four to not be able to go past the blue cones to keep them defending deep. Condition the attacking players to stay inside the Zone 14 orange coned off area so they MUST condense and get tight and get close to each other.

# Getting shots in on goal

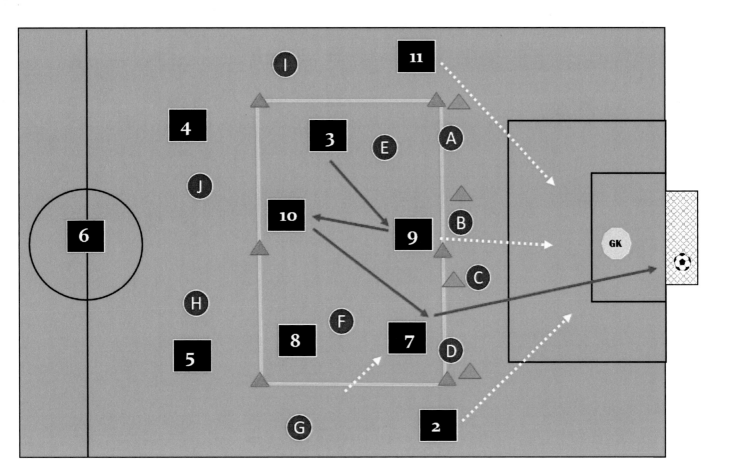

Again short and sharp build up, good positions in tight spaces between opponents and movements OFF the ball to get free to get into a shooting position. Other players follow in for rebounds but time it so they are not offside. Typical Messi run.

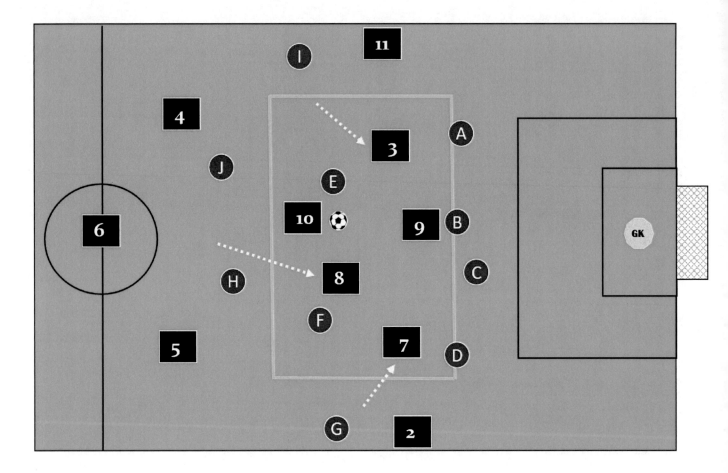

This can be one full session practicing playing short and tight and with quick 1 and 2 touch play. Players must move subtly to get into open very tight passing lanes between opponents. Play quickly.

We want to overload Zone 14 in the center of the field buy maintain two wide players so there is an option to play wide. The idea is to get up in numbers in front of the two center backs. If the fullbacks tuck in to help as they have here and equal the numbers up then we can go wide to (2) and (11).

**When opponents defend deep and there is no space in behind we must "initially" play in front of their back line**

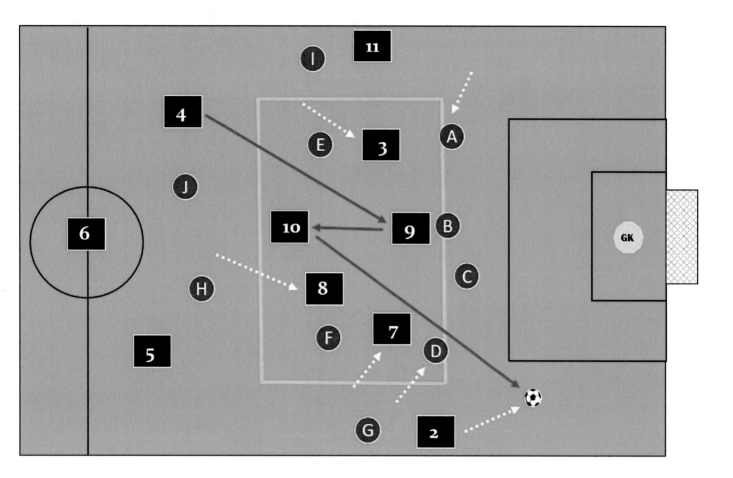

Use (9) as a pivot to set things up. (9) must be strong and able to hold the ball up to bring others into play. We MUST maintain a wide player each side of the field to get them in like above. Here we have 5 players in a very tight area supporting each other.

# Lots of quick passing and moving in the tight area in front of the center backs

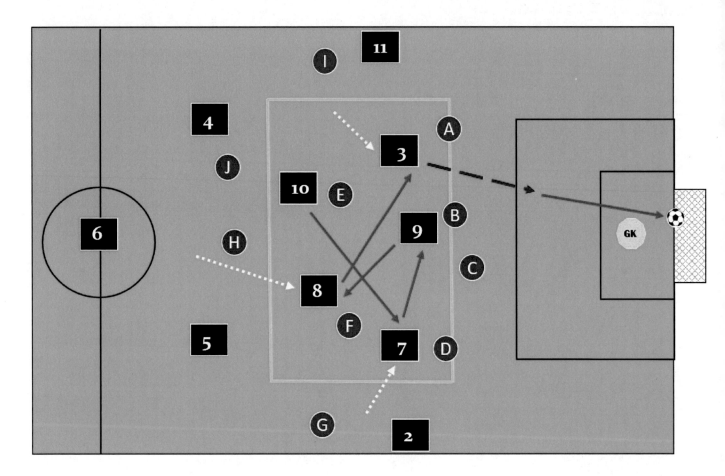

To practice this idea have your main players who would be in this situation working in a 35 x 25 area to get used to playing in tight areas and keeping the ball. Of course opponents midfield players will drop to help out unless we catch them out of position quickly. (3) dribbles through to score. Jordi Alba of Barcelona.

**Pass into the striker and follow and receive back, very simple but effective**

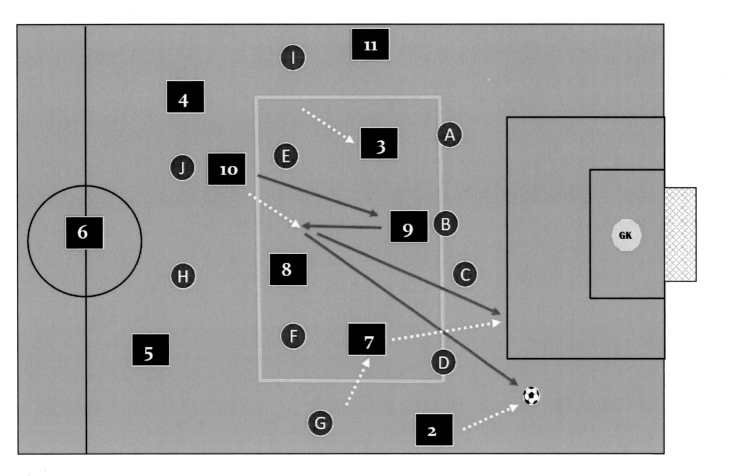

Use (9) as a pivot to set things up. (9) must be strong and able to hold the ball up to bring others into play. We MUST maintain a wide player each side of the field to get them in like above. Pass in, follow, get it back, play (2) or (7) in. Messi makes many runs like this as the number (7) here.

# Pass into the striker and lay off, very simple but effective

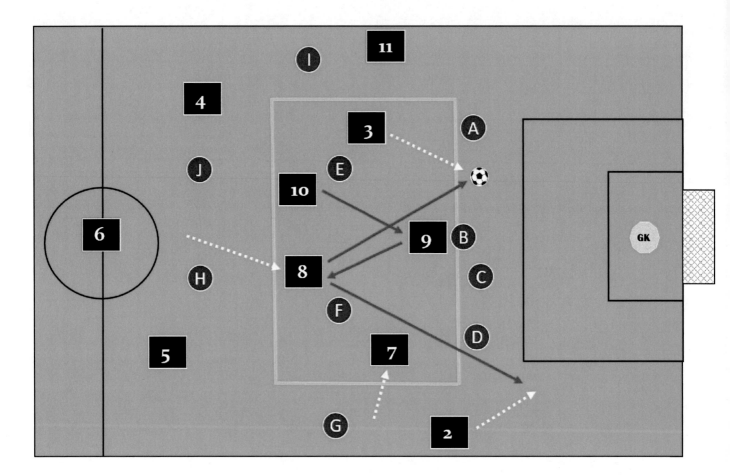

Use (9) as a pivot to set things up. (9) must be strong and able to hold the ball up to bring others into play. Play it off to (8), play (2) or (3) in. Danny Alves of Barcelona makes many runs like this.

# Overloading players in the Zone 14 against a back 5

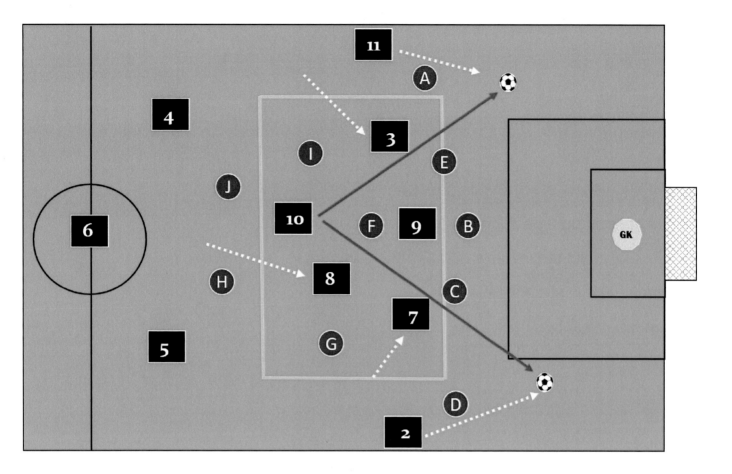

This can be one full session practicing playing short and tight and with quick 1 and 2 touch play. Players must move subtly to get into open very tight passing lanes between opponents. Play quickly.

3 v 3 centrally, 5 in zone 14 in tight spaces keeping the ball, two players offering width one on each side. Looking for diagonal balls in behind the fullbacks to get crosses in. MUST be able to keep possession to make this work.

## Soccer Awareness Rondo: Switching Play using long passes

Area: 30 x 20 or start larger if needed

Three teams of 6 players.

Switching the point of attack with a long pass.

Possession play where in a game you draw players to one side of the field then switch the play quickly.

A great session to practice this concept.

**Develop:** Only outside players can pass a long ball to each other

Must link with middle players to make the switch

Cant tackle the 6 support players

Awareness when two balls are going so players have to observe both to be ready to receive thus improving peripheral vision

# SA Rondo: Switching Play using long passes

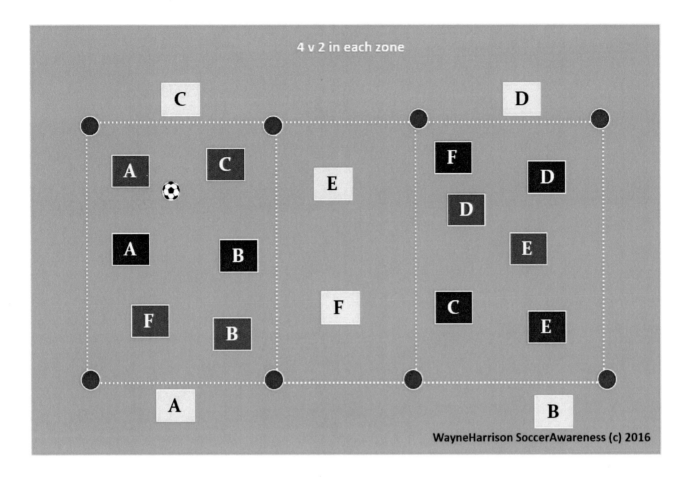

4 v 2 in each zone

WayneHarrison SoccerAwareness (c) 2016

Keeping possession then switching play with a long ball. Do it with one ball initially then with two balls when they get good at it. 4 v 2 means success initially then go 3 v 3.

# Changing the point of attack

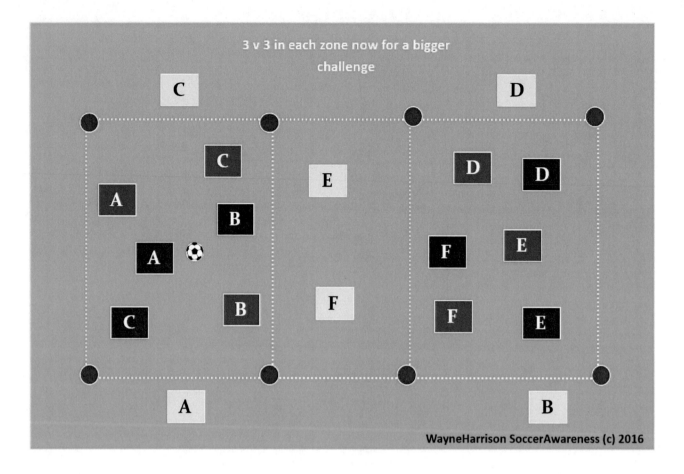

Keeping possession then switching play with a long ball. Do it with one ball initially then with two balls when they get good at it.

# Switching Play using long passes rondo

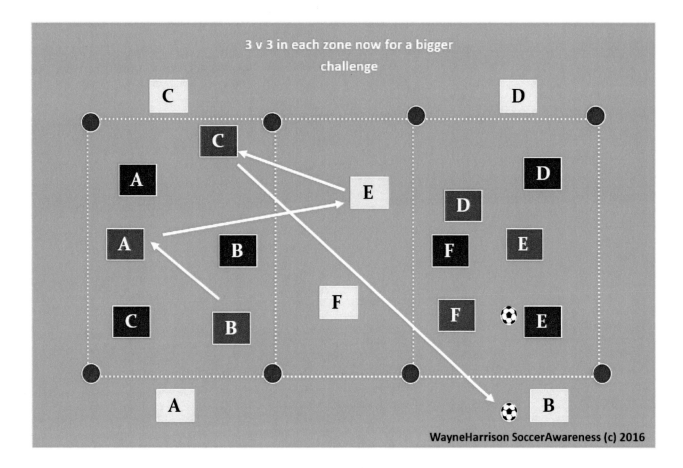

Keeping possession then switching play with a long ball. Now with two balls.. (B) gives it to the blue team and the other ball has to be played immediately into the other side.

## Passing between zones

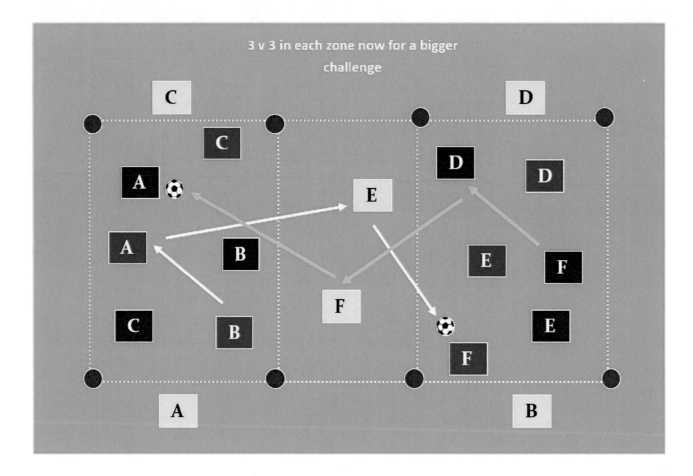

If nothing is on for the long ball then transfer the ball into the other zone.

# Increasing rotation of players

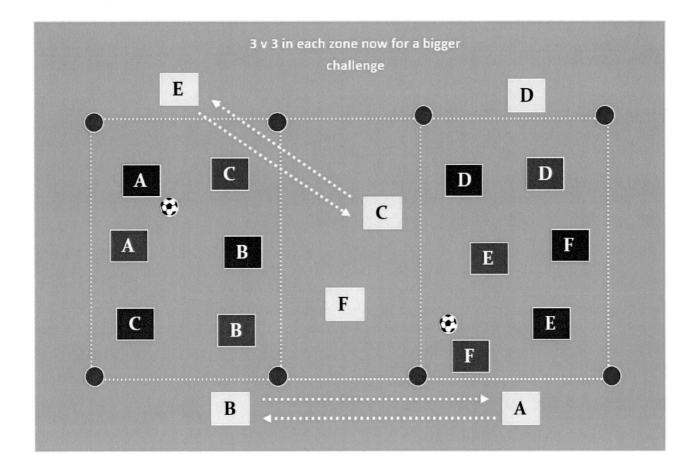

Rotation of the support players changing positions so all players able to move around.

# Circle Rondos: Warm Up: Keep Away 2 Touches

Area: 8 yards by 8 yards

**Progression:** Reduce the size of the Circle to play in smaller spaces to test the players

**Coaching Points:**

1. Keeping the ball away from the central player

2. Passing and maintaining possession

3. Different number of touches (2 touches then 1 touch)

4. Defender must work hard to win the ball; set challenge 10 passes means defender stays in

5. Body position and foot preparation is vital when playing one touch

6. Assessing the next pass before receiving the ball

7. Call the name of the player they are passing to before receiving the ball to show their decision was before receiving the ball

8. Add two then three defenders

# Circle Keep Away Two Touches against 1 player

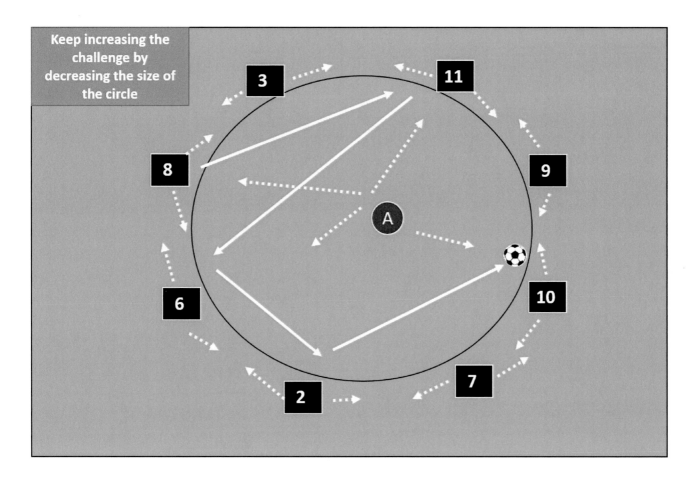

Keep increasing the challenge by decreasing the size of the circle

Players can move on the outside to help each other and open up, a passing lane, just a yard either side can make all the difference.

# Circle Keep Away Two Touches against 2 players

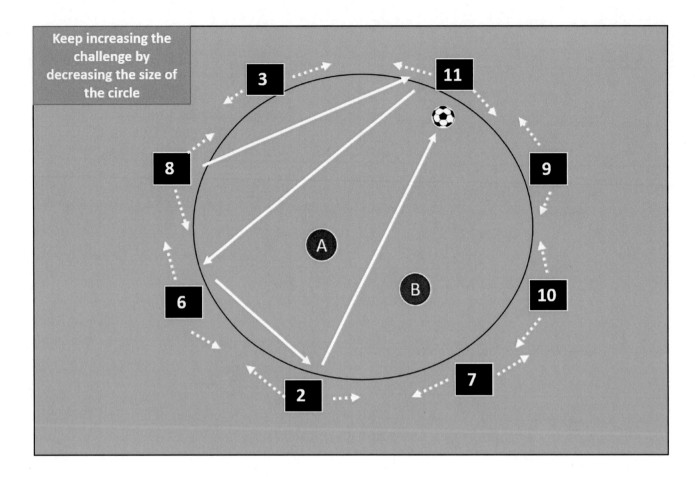

When two defenders are in try to split them with a pass. This is a good warm up for the players and begins the awareness decision making process of rcognizing the pass BEFORE receiving the ball.

# Circle Rondos: Warm Up: Keep Away: 1 Touch only

**Area:** 8 yards by 8 yards

**Progression:** Reduce the size of the Circle to play in smaller spaces to test the players

**Coaching Points:**

1. Keeping the ball away from the central player

2. Passing and maintaining possession

3. Different number of touches (try 2 touches to start)

4. Defender must work hard to win the ball; set challenge 10 passes means defender stays in

5. Body position and foot preparation is vital when playing one touch

6. Assessing the next pass before receiving the ball

7. Call the name of the player they are passing to before receiving the ball to show their decision was before receiving the ball

8. Add two then three defenders

# Warm Up: Circle Keep Away One Touch only against 1 player

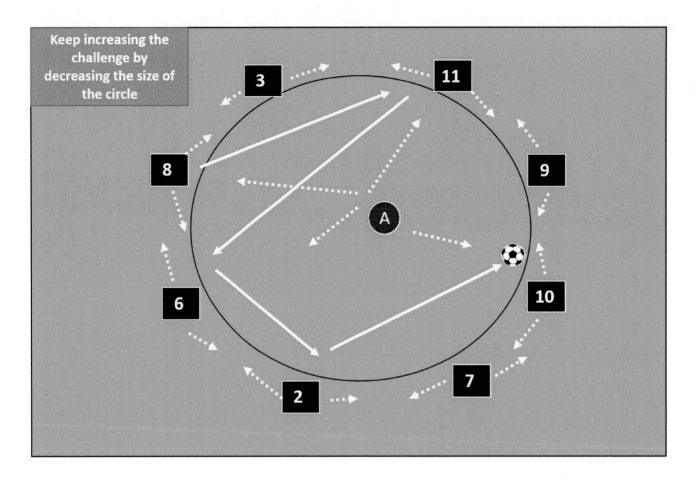

Players can move on the outside to help each other and open up,a passing lane, just a yard either side can make all the difference.

# Warm Up: Circle Keep Away One Touch only against 2 players

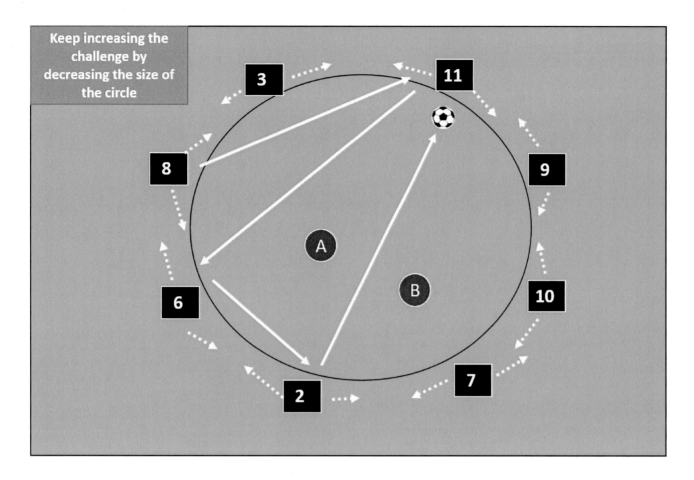

When two defenders are in try to split them with a pass. This is a good warm up for the players and begins the awareness decision making process of rcognizing the pass BEFORE receiving the ball.

# Warm Up: Circle Keep Away One Touch only against 3 players

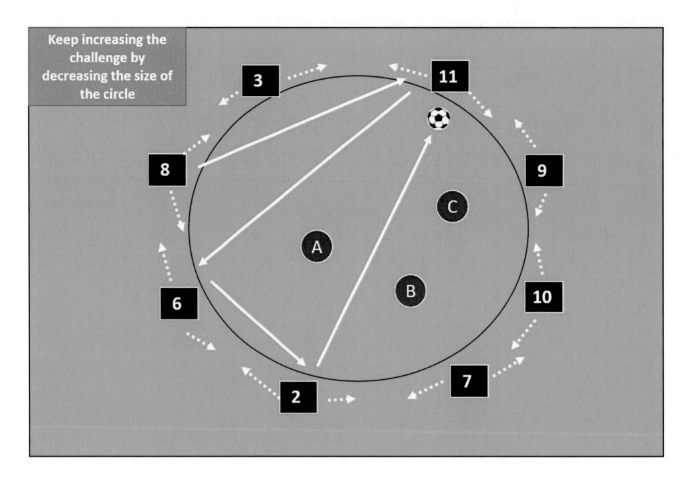

Keep increasing the challenge by decreasing the size of the circle

This is a good warm up for the players and begins the awareness decision making process of rcognizing the pass BEFORE receiving the ball. A bigger challenge with 3 defenders.

# Add an attacking player

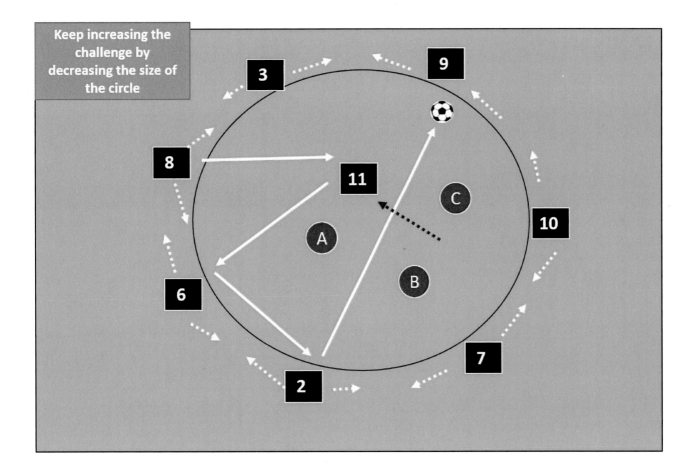

Try to work with the inside player as often as possible. Rotate the defenders and rotate the inside player. (11) has unlimited touches, outside players one touch only.

# Circle Keep away Rondos: Add 2 attacking players (2 touches only)

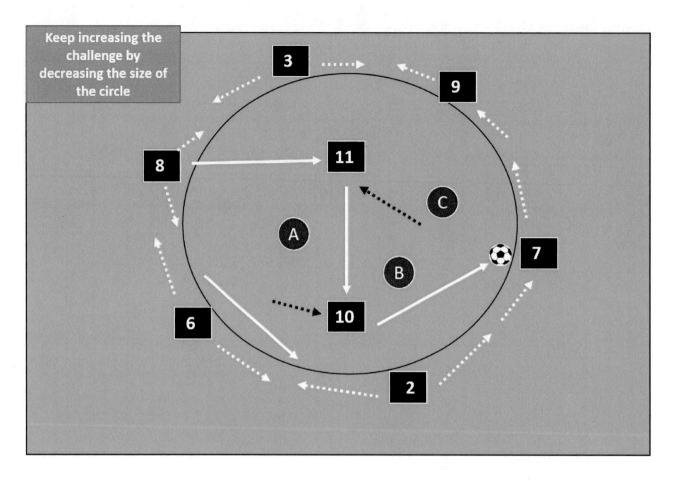

Keep increasing the challenge by decreasing the size of the circle

Two players now playing two touches in the middle the goal is for them to combine and play out of the circle. Now speeding up decision making and movement.

# Circle keep away Rondos: Developing rotation in to out and out to in

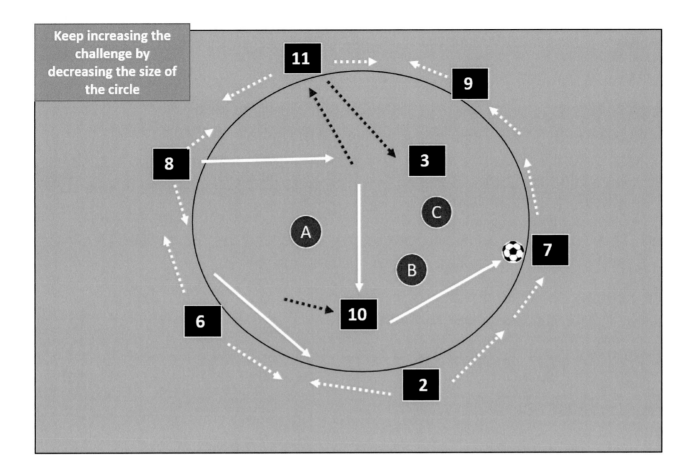

(11) Rotates with (3), (11) going out and (3) coming in. This is an important aspect of play to teach early on as they will start to understand the importance of rotation in the real game situation.

# Circle Rondos: Keep away game working on possession, passing and support; combination plays and rotations of players

All of what we teach in the game is based on the Continuum of development.

We can equate directly the rondo to the training model and what is needed to happen with the C of D.

1. Look and Think: In the circle game players must be looking away from the ball assessing their options. Its easy here as the first player only has two decisions to make, to find the 2nd or 3rd player with a pass so an easy introduction. Try to involve every INSIDE player before passing outside and rotating.

2. Skill: The Decision is made and before the ball arrives the player receiving has assessed the options and has chosen the best one..

3. The Feet are ready; in position before the ball arrives, the back foot being the receiving foot and the player is on their toes.

4. Body position is open due to the back foot receiving of the ball which "forces" the body to open. Receiving player must move their body side to side to get open.

5. Communication: Players should be talking to help each other "in advance" of the ball.

6. Control: If a controlling touch is first but still knowing where the next touch will go.

7. Technique: If playing one touch in the game, a good technique is needed for a successful pass to happen having already made the decision before the ball arrives

8. Tactical Mobility: Now movement in the circle off the ball to get into

9. Mental Transition: A player loses the ball they become a defender and they must move quickly from attacking to defending to try to win the ball back as do his or her teammates.

**Circle Rondos:** Passing and movement warm up: for quick looking and thinking. Various movements to develop decision making with several progressions: An Introduction to all the basics of the thinking process and how it relates to decision making and movement.

# Circle coaching for passing and support

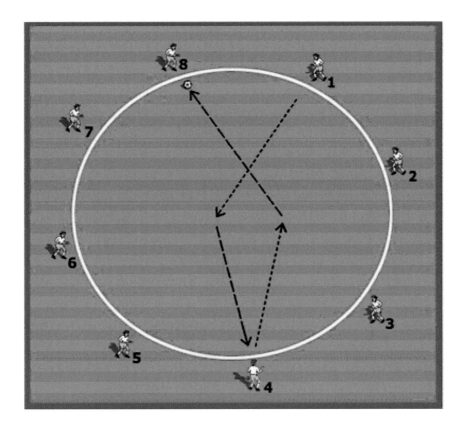

To increase the players awareness instincts ask them to call the name of the player out who they will be passing to, before they receive the ball. This ensures they look to see who is free before they receive the ball so they know in advance who is free to receive.

One ball, (1) runs and passes to (4) and takes their place. (4) Takes the ball, runs and passes to (8) and so on.

**Progression:** Introduce two, then three, then four balls all going at the same time. "Awareness" of where each player is running is needed here so they don't collide and where potential free players to receive are "before" you make the run and pass.

## Coaching Points:

1. Good communication between the players.

2. Quality of the pass (timing, accuracy and weight).

3. Good first touch by the receiver.

4. Progression – Passer becomes a passive defender who puts the receiver under pressure. The receiver must move the ball away at an angle from the pressure on their first touch.

# Running with the ball

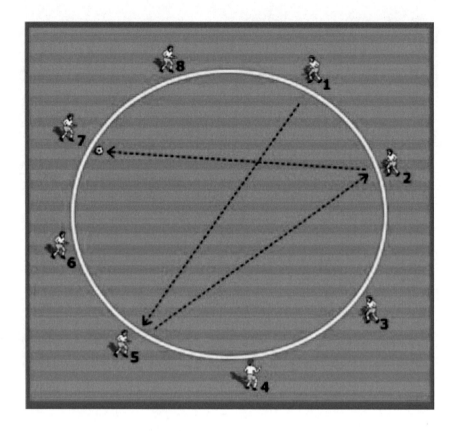

## Running with the ball technique:

1. Head Up – look forward, observing options "before" receiving the ball using the A.I.A. training.

2. Good first touch out of feet, 2-3 touches maximum, not dribbling.

3. Run in a straight line, the quickest route.

4. Running Style, use the front foot to control the ball using the laces.

**Decision:** Where is the player taking the ball? In this case to (5) but (5) must try to decide as the ball is coming not after he or she has it. Identify who is free early.

**Communication:** Call the name of the player you are running the ball to

**Take-overs**

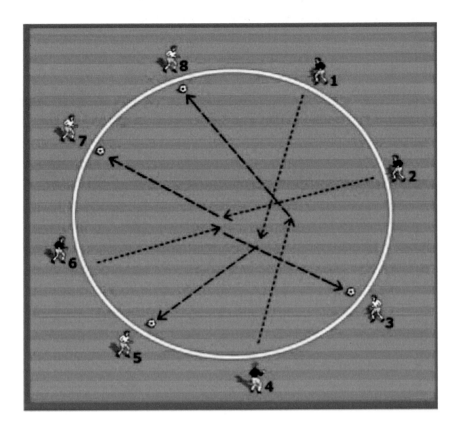

1. You can divide the teams into two and have half the players working and half resting. Work a set time then change the players. Here the players are running with the ball then passing and then will get it back to go somewhere else to another player to work with.

2. Change the emphasis on the movement, running with the ball then during the run the player has to change direction with a clever dribble or turn, or they pass to an outside player, do an overlap around them and get the ball back, play a give and go with them and do a turn when they receive it back.

3. Many ways to develop this idea to get lots of touches on the ball, practicing running with the ball, receiving and turning with the ball and dribbling with the ball, combination plays, give and go's, overlap runs and so on. The coach can use his or her imagination to make this work.

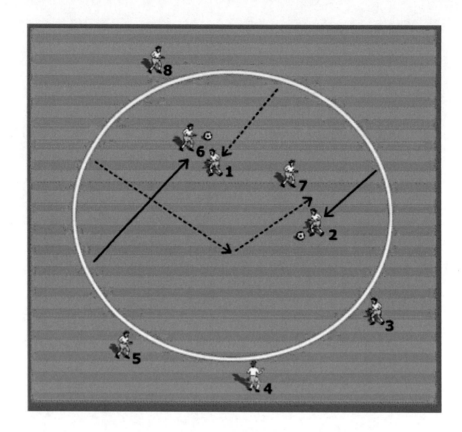

**Progression:** Take-over plays between the players. (1) Runs with the ball makes eye or verbal contact with (6) who comes to meet the ball.

**Coaching Points :**

**Running with the ball technique:**

1. Head Up – look forward, observing options "before" receiving the ball using the Awareness training.

2. Good first touch out of feet, 2-3 touches maximum, not dribbling.

3. Run in a straight line, the quickest route.

4. Running Style, use the front foot to control the ball using the laces.

**Communication;** the player with the ball can dictate who takes it with simple calls (take it, leave it).

Timing of take-over, screen the ball, use the inside foot, change pace, in slow, out quick. Above, (1) does not pass the ball to (6) but allows (6) to take it using the momentum of the ball (if (6) decides to take the ball and they do not do a decoy

# Playing 1 – 2's

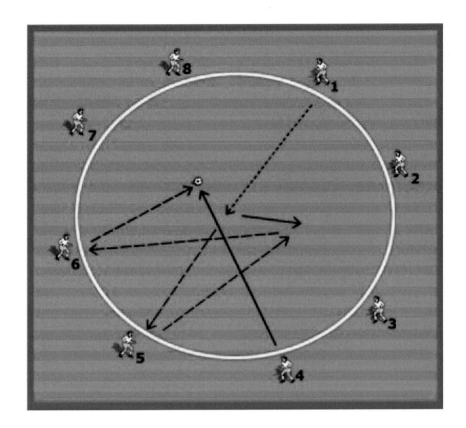

(1) runs with the ball and passes to (6) that plays a 1 – 2 then (1) passes to (5) who carries the move on. (1) Takes (5)'s place.

**Progression:** Use two balls at the same time. Awareness of other players in the same spaces comes into play in the movement of the inside players.

Coaching Points as in previous exercise.

If (1) passes to (6) and supports to the right of (6) then the pass is going to the left to (5) making sure we are working angles of support and passing and it lets (5) know the next pass is going there.

# Third Man Runs

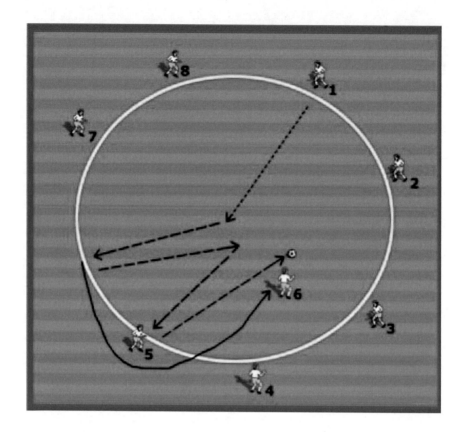

(1) runs with the ball and plays a 1 – 2 with (5), and then passes to (6), at this moment (4) makes a run to receive the ball off (6)'s pass.

(1) takes (4)'s place. This exercise is about movement off the ball thinking a move ahead of the game.

**Coaching Points** as previously but includes:

1. Timing of the support run off the ball to receive the pass.

2. Timing of the pass into space not to feet.

3. Initially when the player passes back always go to the same side (right or left) to get the players into the routine.

# Overlap Runs

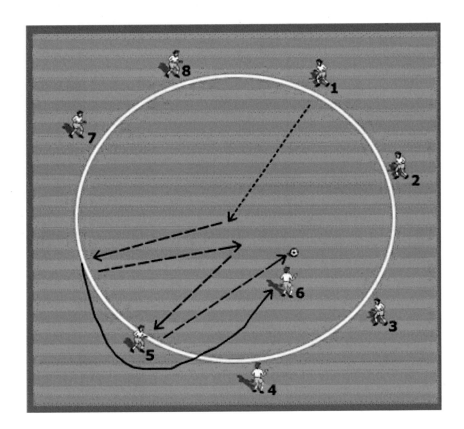

(1) runs with the ball and plays a 1 – 2 with (6), then lays the ball off to (5). At the same time (6) makes an overlap run around (5) to receive the pass in front. (1) Takes the place of (6). Develop the usual way. Coaching Points as the previous exercise but this time the support run is in the form of an overlap. Timing of the overlap run is important as is the timing of the pass into space in front of the overlapping player to receive.

# Passing and Support

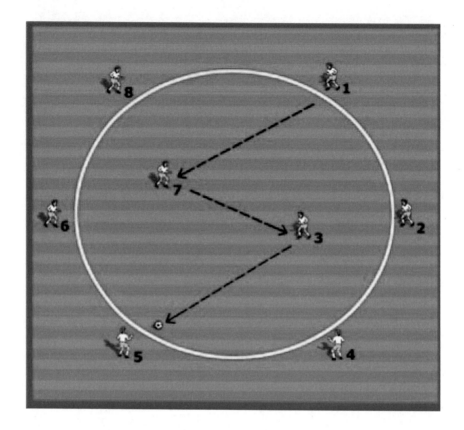

As the ball is going to (7) he or she have already looked to see where (3) is to pass to. (3) Has already got into a support position to be ready to help (7) and at the same time is viewing the field to see who is available to receive a pass on the outside. As the ball travels to (3) ask them to call the name of the player they intend to pass to, before the ball gets to their feet. To do this they need to look at (7) as the ball arrives, look to see who is free then look back to see the ball coming.

(7) moves to an angled support position to receive the pass from (1). (3) Makes an angle off (7) to receive the ball then passes to (5).

## Coaching Points:

1. Body shape when receiving;

2. Quality of pass (weight, timing and accuracy)

3. Support angles

4. Good first touch.

# Passing and Support

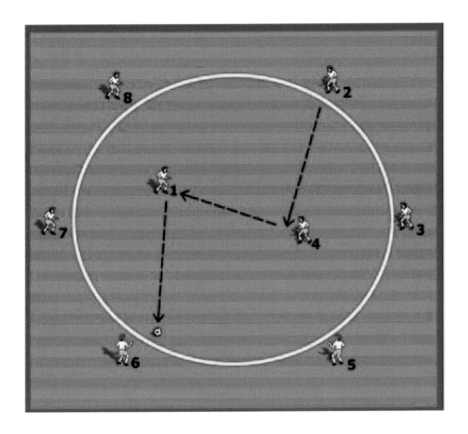

## Progression:

1. Three players working together in the middle

2. Two pairs working together in the middle.

Pass in the same sequence each time into the middle players, awareness required as to where players are on the outside and also, or more particularly, in the middle where they can get in the way of each other in the two team situation.

(4) moves to an angled support position to receive from (2). (1) Makes an angle off (4) to receive then pass to (6).

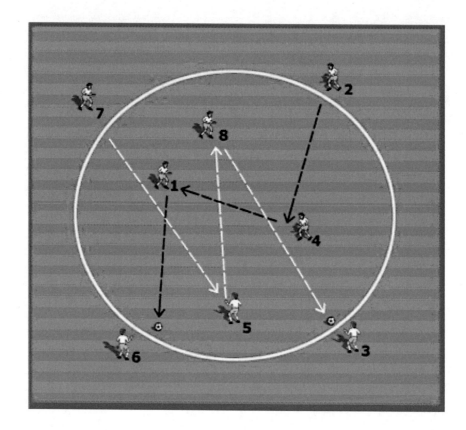

(4) moves to an angled support position to receive from (2). (1) Makes an angle off (4) to receive then pass to (6).

**Coaching Points:**

1. Body shape when receiving.

2. Quality (weight and accuracy) of pass.

3. Support angles.

4. Good first touch.

**Progression:**

1. Three players working together in the middle. Try one touch and two touch play.

2. Two pairs working in the middle with a ball each pair.

Creating awareness of where the other pair is causing players to look away from the ball and observe their surroundings.

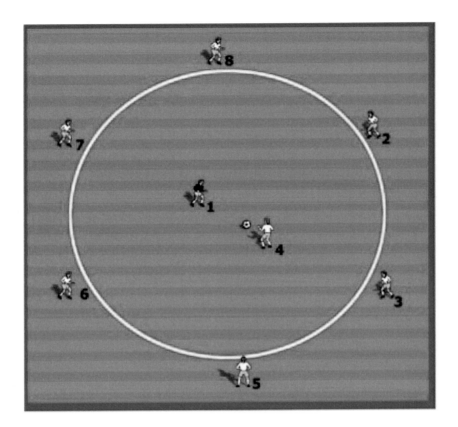

## Introduce Opponents

1. 1 v 1's – This is now possession play (keep ball) in the middle to start, outside players two touch but must release it quickly to keep the pressure on inside the circle. This is high intensive work. Rotate players. Inside players as many touches as they like, practicing dribbling skills in 1 v 1 situations, passing and movement off the ball working combinations with team mates.

2. Inside players cannot tackle outside players but can intercept passes from them. Outside players can move side to side to improve their support angles. Emphasize passing to both space and to feet.

3. This is technically a 7 v 1 in favor of the player in possession.

4. A 2 v 1's - Two then one touch on the outside. You can work on attacking players passing and support techniques or the sole defender on defensive skills.

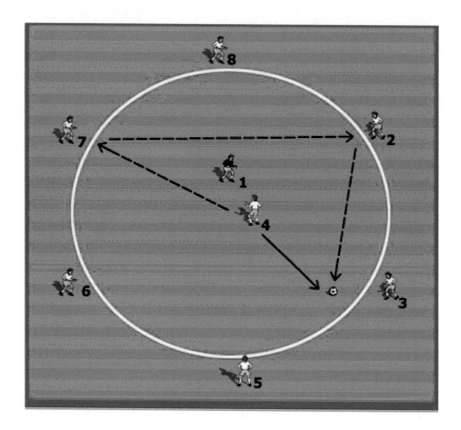

1. Players can pass the ball around the outside until a pass is on to an inside player. You can restrict the number of continuous outside passes as the main work has to be done by the inside players so keeping them involved.

2. Players on the outside identify who they are passing to as the ball is coming to them. They can call a players name to pass to "before" they get it so the inside player in possession knows which player to work off next to receive the ball from again. Or as the ball is coming to (7), player (2) may call and ask for the next pass to make (7) aware that this player is open and available, good communication is the key to this.

3. Here (4) passes to (7), who, as the ball is traveling calls out (2)'s name. This is a cue for (4) to then change position to receive the next pass from (2) early and in space. One or two touch play on the outside will mean this is quick passing and it will help (4) get possession again early and in space away from defender (1), who hopefully has been left flat footed.

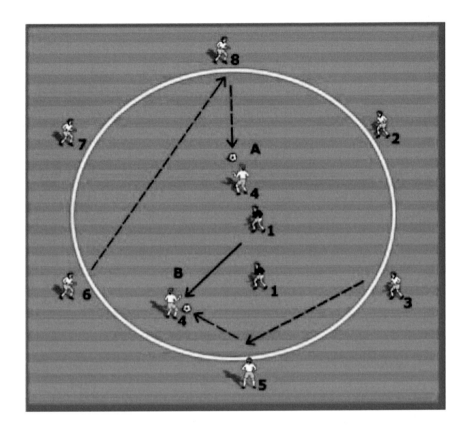

1. Avoid players closing their own space down by getting too close to the player on the ball. At figure 1, (4) has got too close but also gone in too straight so cannot view the full field nor see where the defender is.

2. Correct movement would be off at an angle to receive facing forward and inside if possible seeing the whole field. Figure 2 shows this. If the defender blocks the pass to (4) then the passing channel is open for (5) to pass elsewhere and (4) will work their position off the next pass.

3. Try to receive the ball facing inside not outside the circle so you can see the full area and all of the players if possible. An open body stance will help this even receiving "side-on" helps. In figure A (4) can see (8) but little else of the other players or the field, in figure B, (4) can see most of the players and most of the field when receiving the ball or moving to receive the next pass if (3) passes it elsewhere.

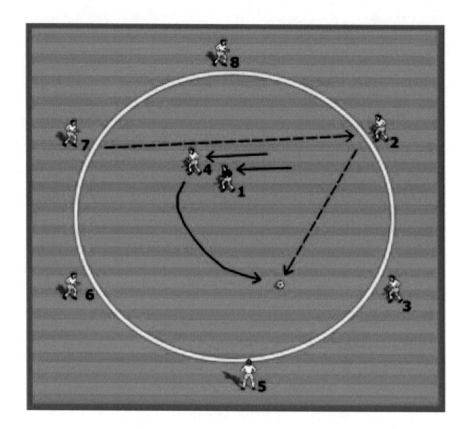

1. Here (4) comes to receive a pass, (1) is marking tightly. (7) Can pass the ball to the opposite side of (4) away from the side (1) is defending.

2. (7) can also put a little more weight on the pass, (4) lets it run across his or her body with a feint to fool (1), it runs to (2) who then can lay the ball off back to (40 who has turned away from (10 to get free to receive the next pass.

3. This movement creates space behind for (4) to run into off the next pass. (4) has to be aware of the position of (2) "before" the pass so as to let it run to them. (2) Has to be ready to receive and expect the ball from (7).

4. A one or two touch pass from (2) into space for (4) ensures the movement and passing is rapid and gives the defender (1) less time to react.

5. Try to get faced up to the defender when you receive the ball and not play with your back to them this gives the player on the ball the advantage.

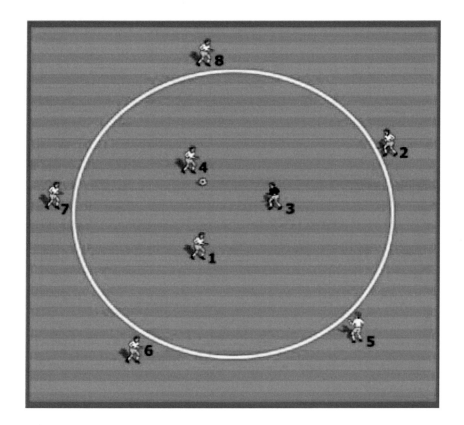

1. Here we have an overload of a 2 v 1 in the middle. (1) And (4) must keep the ball away from (3) using the outside players as support.

2. If (3) wins the ball then as incentives have that player use the outside players to try to keep possession.

3. Develop: If an inside player gives the ball away, that player then becomes the defender against the other two players.

4. Players (1) and (4) must make it as difficult as possible for defender (3) to win the ball. If it becomes too easy using the outside players then limit them to one touch each and have the two inside players limited to two touches then one touch so the challenge becomes greater.

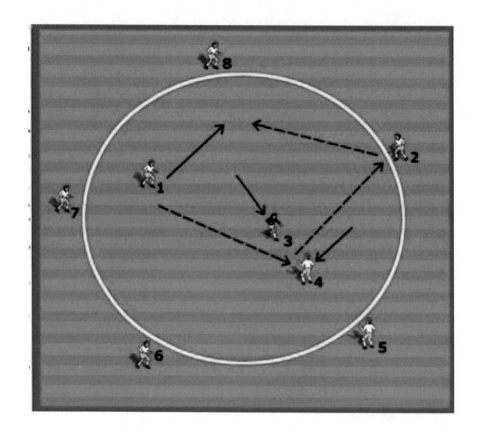

1. You can also limit the number of times the ball is played around the outside players so it has to come back into an inside player every two passes for example. Play around with this until you can get a balanced situation putting the two inside players under enough pressure with restrictions, to make it demanding but also giving the defender a fair chance to win the ball back.

2. Here (4) creates an angle for the pass from (1) by moving into space (1) can see. (4) Then lays a pass off to (2) who passes into space to draw (1) to the ball and take him or her away from (3). Too often player (4) may stand in a position behind (3) so (1) can't see them. This really emphasized the need for movement off the ball to support a player on it.

3. Awareness instincts being trained here again for all the players both in the middle and on the outside. As the ball is traveling to (4) he or she needs to call the name of the player they are passing to before they receive it, then (4) has to be aware of where to pass it next, in this case into space for (1).

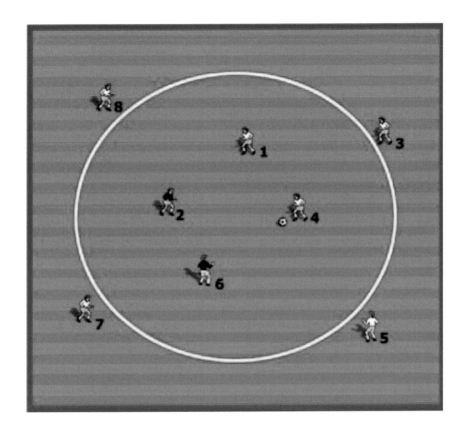

1. A 2 v 2's - (1) and (4) against (2) and (6). Building to a 3 v 2 and so on depending on numbers you are working with. Using outside players as support men for both teams.

2. Inside players can have free play then develop to three then two touch to improve speed of decision making.

3. Outside players two touch then one touch play.

4. This is technically a 4 v 2 in favor of the team in possession.

5. Keep rotating players putting them with different partners to work with. This is physical work but players get a break on the outside to recover ensuring quality work inside the circle.

6. An alternative is to have two teams and the inside players can only pass to their team mates on the outside, this is giving them fewer choices and increasing the difficulty of the exercise.

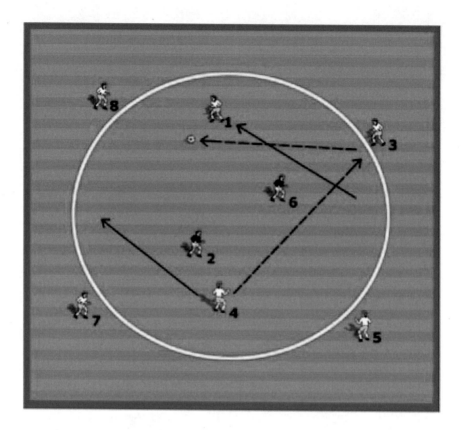

1. Using the outside players – an example would be as above where (1) has gotten into the same passing lane as (3). (1) Shapes up to receive a pass but lets it run across the body through to (3) and then makes a movement to support the next pass from (3).

2. This results in dummying defender (6) into thinking (1) will receive the ball and so (2) pressures (4). The movement results in (1) getting free from the marking of defender (6) using (3) to receive the next pass into space.

3. In the meantime (4) will be on the move to support the next pass from (1) and thus getting away from the marking of defender (2).

4. Initially have no restriction on the passing so the players can pass around the outside of the circle until an inside player is available to receive the ball.

5. Progression - As the players improve put conditions in where there can be only three, then two passes between outside players, then the ball must be passed to an inside player. The two inside players must link up with a pass before the ball goes to an outside player again.

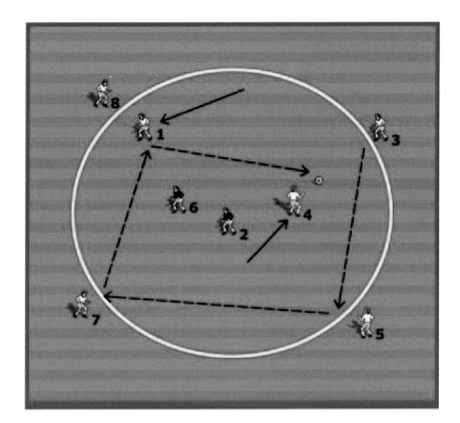

1. The ball is being passed around the outside of the circle. After two passes it must go to an inside player. The inside players have to work hard to get into a position to receive the pass knowing the next pass has to be inside to one of them. Create a triangle of support between the two players in the middle and the outside player you are working with.

2. If it is (1), as above, who receives the pass, then (4) must work off the ball to get into a position to support (1) particularly if the condition is that a pass must be made inside the circle between the two inside players before it can go out again.

3. This is a great session for working on movement off the ball for players to support each other in tight spaces as well as developing technical skills on the ball in tight spaces.

4. Introduce a free player who works with both teams when in possession to develop the practice into a 3 v 2.

# Circle keep away: Two teams: 1 v 1

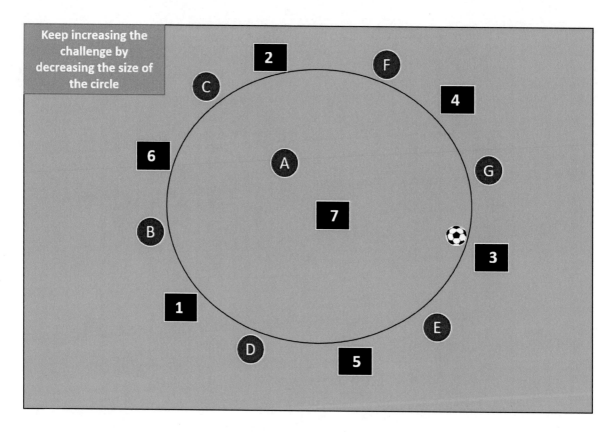

Eight players or more can do this. Circle can be 20 yards across, you can only pass to your own team. Player for 2 minutes then rotate players.

# Circle keep away: Two teams: 1 v 1

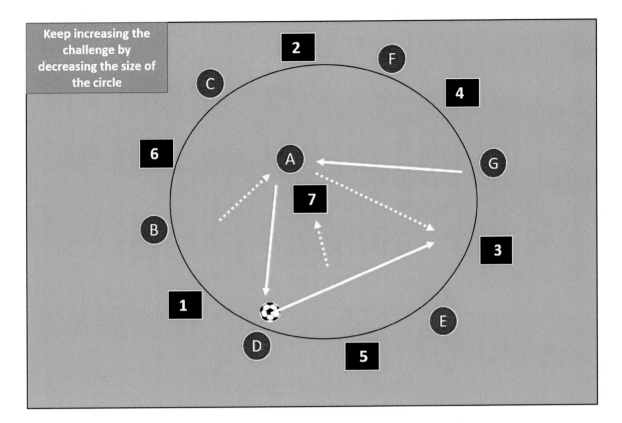

Keep increasing the challenge by decreasing the size of the circle

(A) Can pass and move or dribble and beat (7) 1 v 1. In this case working on a 1 touch pass and move.

## Give and go combination: Two teams: 1 v 1

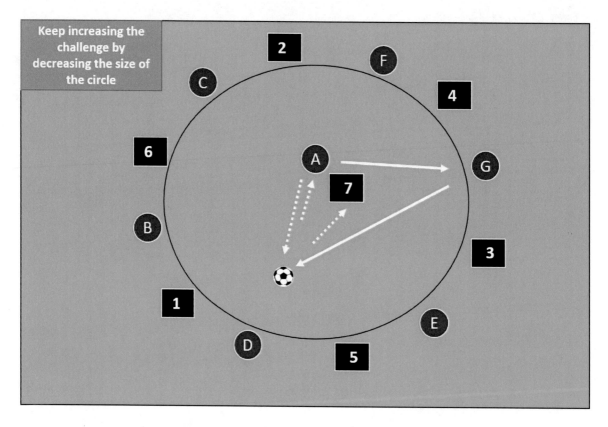

Playing give and goes. (A) draws (7) to the ball and plays a give and go off (G).

# Dummy run: Two teams: 1 v 1

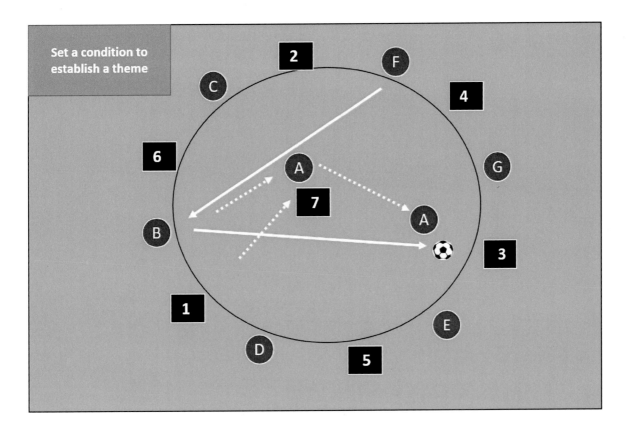

Inside Players can use the outside players to dummy the defender. (A) moves to receive off (F) but lets the ball run past them to (B), (A) then spins away to get the next pass off (B).

# Third man run: Two teams: 1 v 1

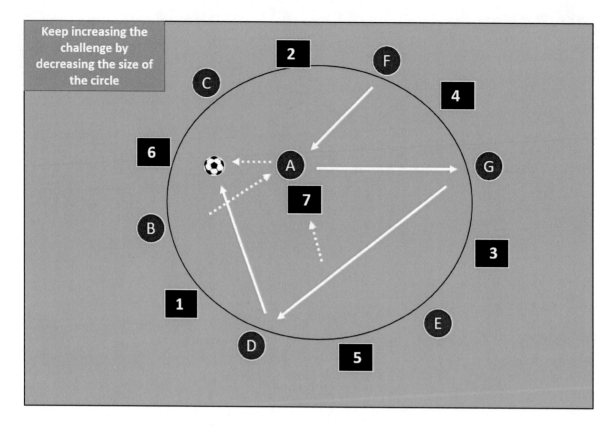

Now (A) doesnt receive it directly off the player he or she passed to but off another player (D). (A) now performs a third man run OFF the ball to receive and continue in possession.

# Circle keep away: Two teams: 2 v 2

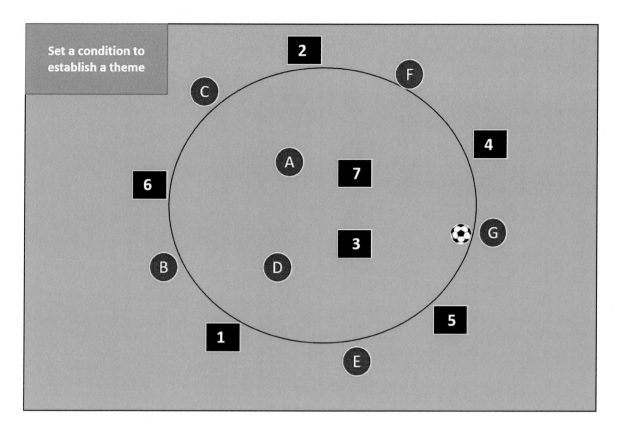

Set a condition to establish a theme

2 v 2 using the outside players to rotate in and out. A great exercise to get players to interchange positions.

## Circle keep away: Two teams: 2 v 2

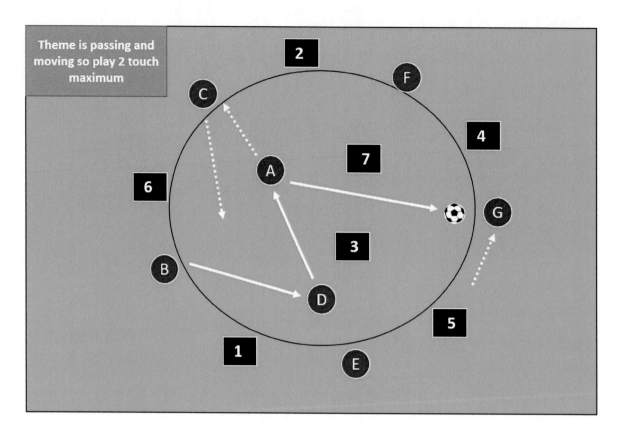

Try to open up passing lanes between the opponents. Here (A) plays the pass between (7) and (5) and then rotates out with (C).

# Circle keep away: Two teams: 2 v 2

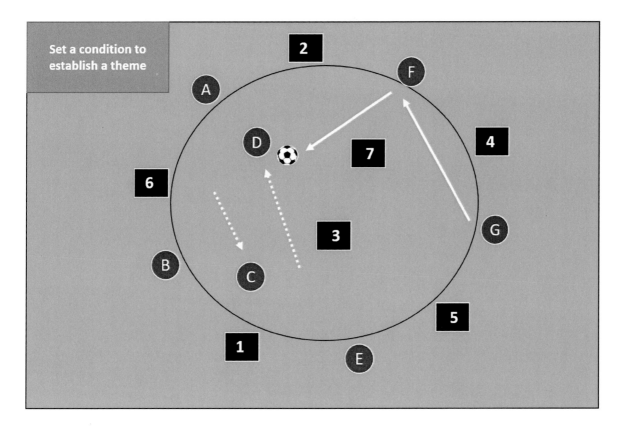

Set a condition to establish a theme

Constantly changing players on the inside which teaches them to get the good habit of movement on the field and changing traditional positional ideas.

# Circle keep away: Two teams: 3 v 3 (Part 1)

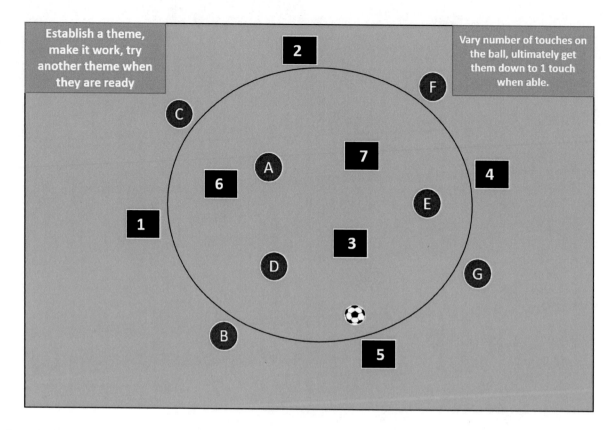

Now 3 v 3, less space, one players rotates out leaving two in. Those two must be getting into passing lanes to offer up 2 options for the player bringing the ball in next.

# Circle keep away: Two teams: 3 v 3 (Part 2)

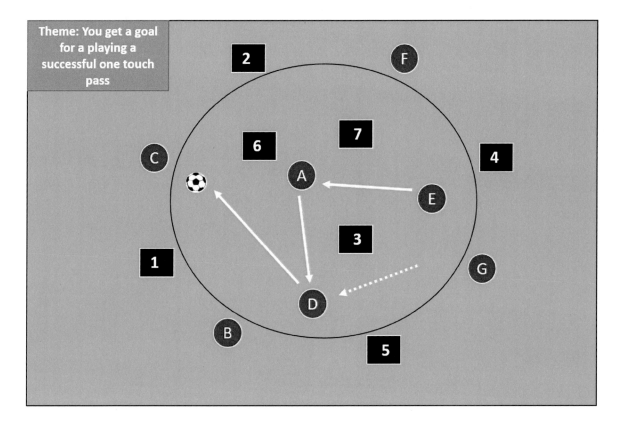

**Theme: You get a goal for a playing a successful one touch pass**

Now 3 v 3, less space, one players rotates out leaving two in. Those two must be getting into passing lanes to offer up 2 options for the player bringing the ball in next.

## Circle keep away: Two teams: 3 v 3 (Part 3)

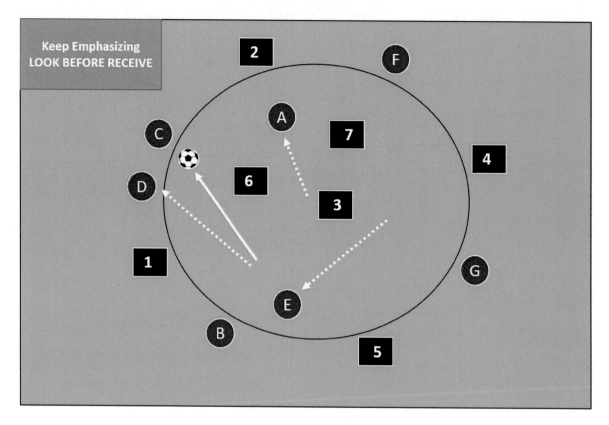

Here (C) receives the ball. (C) should have already LOOKED to see what the next option might be BEFORE receiving the ball.

# Circle keep away: Two teams: 3 v 3 (Part 4)

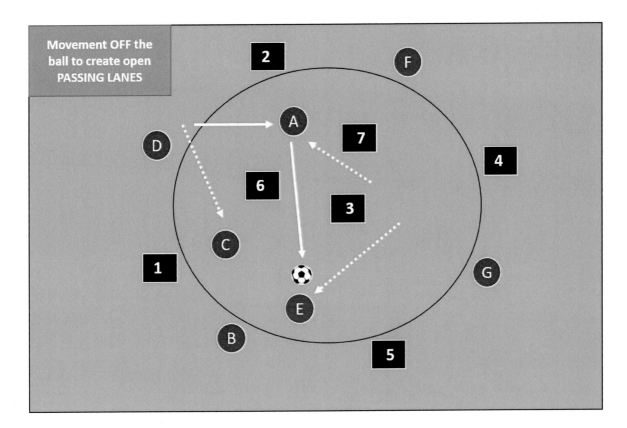

Likewise (A) and (E) should already be on the move (as shown above) to open up passing lanes for (C) to play the ball in, even one touch if possible for speed of play.

# Circle keep away: Two teams: 3 v 3 (Part 5)

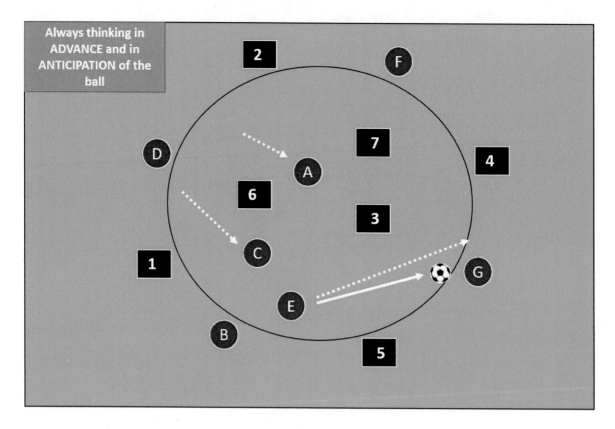

(E) Passes to (G) who can bring it in and play one or two touches. (C) has moved into space to become available. (A) has moved to open up for (C) or directly from (G).

# Circle keep away: Two teams: 3 v 3 (Part 6)

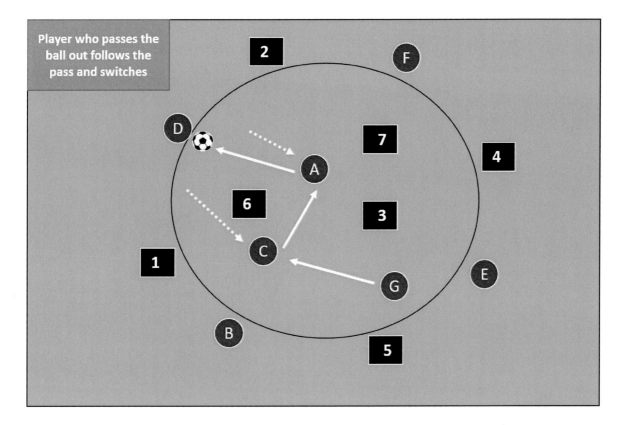

Player who passes the ball out follows the pass and switches

(E) Passes to (G) who can bring it in and play one or two touches. (C) has moved into space to become available. (A) has moved to open up for (C) or directly from (G).

Try to involve every INSIDE player before passing outside and rotating.

# Circle keep away: Two teams: 3 v 3 (Part 7)

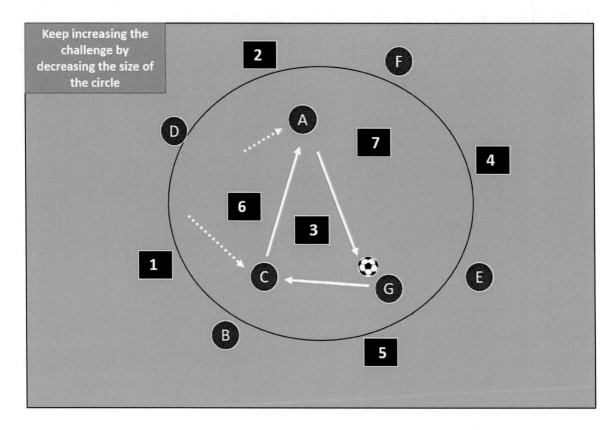

Players can pass and maintain possession inside if the situation if available to do so. The game is a small scale version of what we do in the real game pass and move, rotate positions, keep possession.

# Rotating OFF the ball: Two teams: 3 v 3 (Part 8)

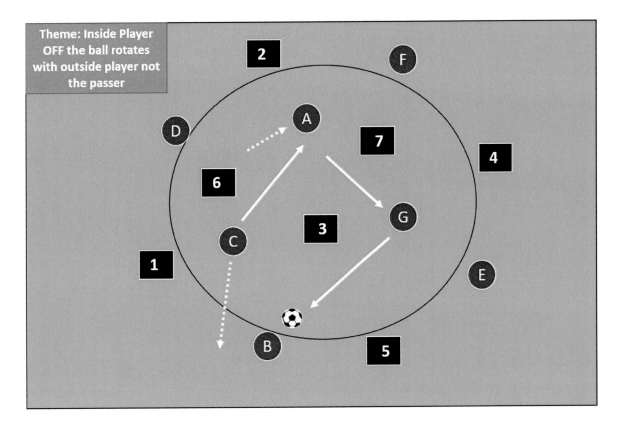

Now it is NOT the passer who rotates outside it is another of the players doing so..Here (C) rotates even though (G) made the pass. (B) brings the abll in and works with (A) and (G). Good vision and communication is needed here.

## Introduce Combination plays: Two teams: 3 v 3 (Part 9)

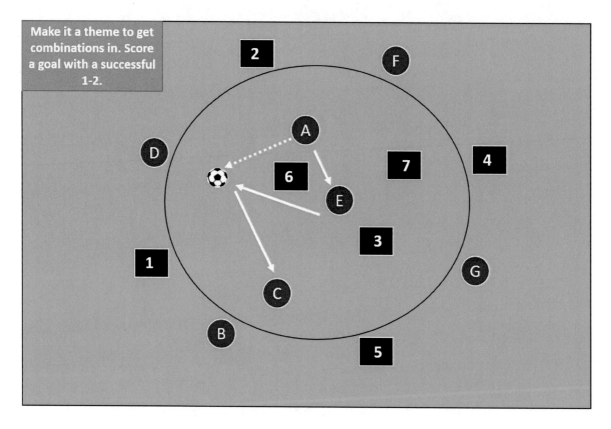

We can get many different ideas of combination plays within the circle here are a few suggestions we can try. Playing give and goes (1-2s) inside the circle.

# A Third Man Run: Two teams: 3 v 3 (Part 10)

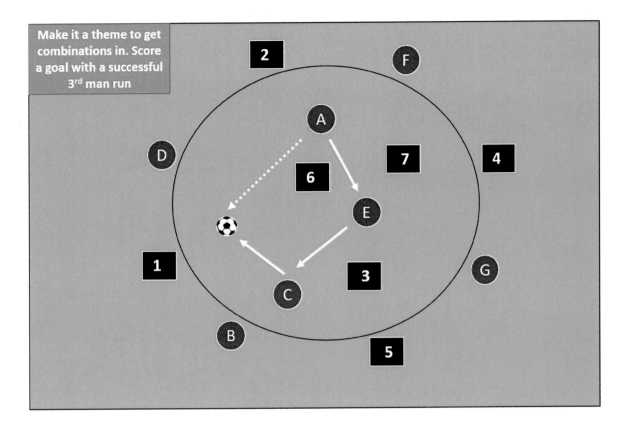

Make it a theme to get combinations in. Score a goal with a successful 3rd man run

A third man run off the ball by (A) who started the move.

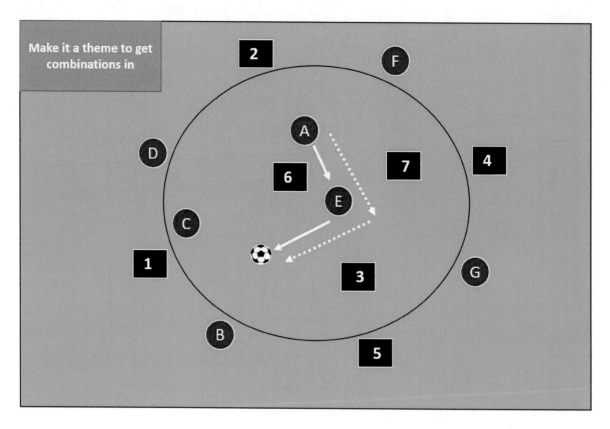

Now (A) performs an overlap run with (E). Good communication is needed here.

# Decoy overlap run: Two teams: 3 v 3 (Part 12)

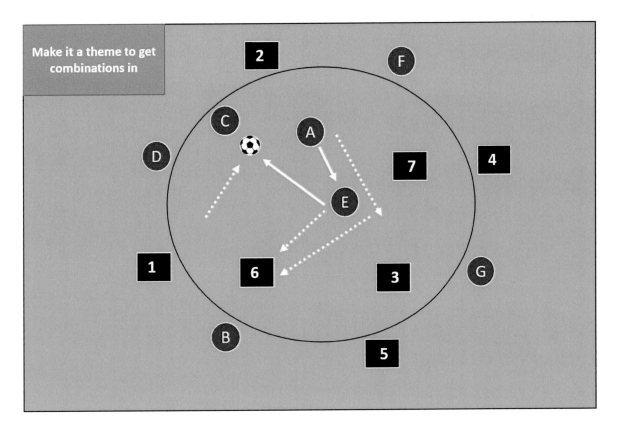

Make it a theme to get combinations in

(6) Tracks the run of (A) making the overlap and closes the space down so (E) passes to (C) instead using (A) as a decoy.

## Add a Neutral player: Two teams: 3 v 3 + 1 (Part 13)

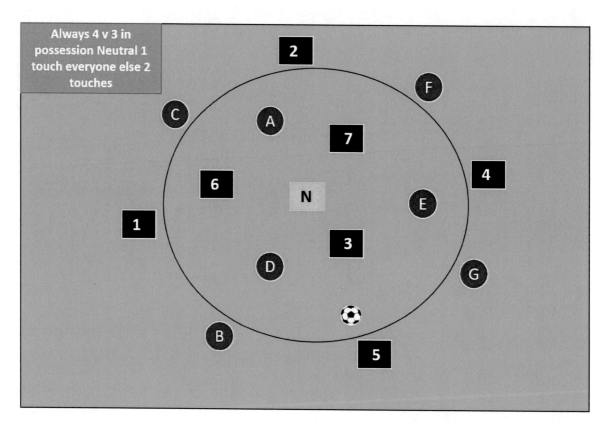

Now 3 v 3 plus 1 neutral player to aid each team. Can vary the number of touches on the neutral player I like to restrict them to one touch to really test them.

# In Conclusion

Rondos come in many shapes and forms, circles, squares; diamonds and so on but they all have the same meaning, to increase the speed of decision making, improve the technique of each player building it up to a pressured situation; to improve the tactical awareness of players, teach them in the art of good positioning on the field, moving into open passing lanes to help each other; and to develop a possession based game for your team.

The better we get at possessing the ball (which Rondos can play a massive part in teaching) the more likely we are to win games, not guaranteed; but it certainly helps.

The best form of defense is attack so the best form of defense is winning the ball and keeping it so we defend less.

A major use of a Rondo also is teaching players how to play WITHOUT the ball, that is positioning OFF the ball. Whilst the obvious focus is on keeping the ball and developing skill to do that, Rondos also by their very nature develop soccer intelligence off the ball as well as on it.

We hope we have given you food for thought with this presentation and encouraged you to not only use these ideas but to improve on them and change them to suit your players needs.

The game is always evolving and rondos can evolve and improve also through each coaches imagination.

Kindest Regards, Wayne Harrison of Soccer Awareness

# ABOUT WAYNE HARRISON

Married to Mary for 30 years with two daughters Sophie 26 and Johanna 23.

Wayne is available for Soccer Symposiums and Conventions wherever they are needed; and able to offer field clinics and classroom presentations of your choosing. He has vast experience in this field of work.

His specialist system of play is the 4-2-3-1. His favored type of development training is that of creating the "THINKING PLAYER" through his SOCCER AWARENESS methods of coaching.

His belief is developing the MIND of the player through ONE TOUCH training, which is purely to help the development of the SKILL FACTOR (the when, where how and why of decision making; or the thinking process). He wants all coaches to teach where it is the player who becomes the decision maker not the coach.

You can contact him on soccerawareness@outlook.com and / or view his website www.soccerawareness.com.

This book was reproduced in partnership with Amplified Soccer Marketing, LLC. Find out more at www.amplifiedsoccer.com.

# GET THESE ADDITIONAL BOOKS AT
## WWW.SOCCERAWARENESS.COM

**Wayne Harrison** presents **Exclusive eBook Series**

**Soccer Awareness Training**

Tactical Thoughts on the Development of the New 4 v 4, 7 v 7 and 9 v 9 Game Sizes

**Wayne Harrison** presents **Exclusive eBook Series**

**eBook 25**

How to Play the 4-2-3-1: Attacking and Defensive Positioning

**Wayne Harrison** presents **Exclusive eBook Series**

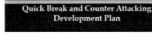

**eBook 22**

Quick Break and Counter Attacking Development Plan

**Wayne Harrison** presents **Exclusive eBook Series**

**eBook 20**

Connecting Small Sided Games with 8 v 8 and 11 v 11

**Wayne Harrison** presents **Exclusive eBook Series**

**eBook 13**

17 Best Warm Ups

**Wayne Harrison** presents **Exclusive eBook Series**

**eBook 12**

16 Team Shape Games
Based On Age Group Sizes Of Games

**Wayne Harrison** presents **Exclusive eBook Series**

**eBook 6**

Sideways On or Facing Forward Body Shape for Striker Position; The Brazilian Way

**Wayne Harrison** presents **Exclusive Book Series**

**eBook 31:**

Developing the Four Phases of the Game

**Wayne Harrison** presents **Exclusive eBook Series**

**eBook 19**

The Principles of Defending for U8 to U14

# GET THESE ADDITIONAL BOOKS AT
## WWW.SOCCERAWARENESS.COM

**Wayne Harrison**
presents
**Exclusive eBook Series**

### eBook 18

Identifying and Solving Common Game
Situation Problems in the
Training Environment

**Wayne Harrison**
presents
**Exclusive eBook Series**

### eBook 16:

Soccer Awareness "One Touch" Training:
Developing its Relationship with
Movement Off the Ball

**Wayne Harrison**
presents
**Exclusive eBook Series**

### eBook 11

Turning Technique And Skill
For 6 To 10 Year Olds

**Wayne Harrison**
presents
**Exclusive Book Series**

### eBook 8:

Small-Sided Games for Strikers

**Wayne Harrison**
presents
**Exclusive Book Series**

### eBook 7:

17 Shooting Practices for U6 to U10

**Wayne Harrison**
presents
**Exclusive eBook Series**

### eBook 5

Attacking Combination Plays

**Wayne Harrison**
presents
**Exclusive eBook Series**

### eBook 4

Attacking and Defending Games:
Challenging the Mindset and Mental
Transition of the Players

**Wayne Harrison**
presents
**Exclusive eBook Series**

### eBook 3

33 Passing And Receiving Practices
For U6 To U10

**Wayne Harrison**
presents
**Exclusive eBook Series**

### eBook Two:

12 Dynamic Target Games for Soccer

Made in the USA
San Bernardino, CA
17 October 2016